ORGANIC
Wire and Metal Jewelry

Stunning Pieces Made with Sea Glass, Stones, and Crystals

Beth L. Martin
Eva M. Sherman

Kalmbach Books
21027 Crossroads Circle
Waukesha, Wisconsin 53186
www.Kalmbach.com/Books

© 2014 Beth L. Martin and Eva M. Sherman

Published in 2014
18 17 16 15 14   1 2 3 4 5

Manufactured in the United States of America

ISBN: 978-0-87116-704-0
EISBN: 978-1-62700-107-6

Editor: Erica Swanson
Art Director: Lisa Bergman
Photographer: William Zuback

Publisher's Cataloging-in-Publication Data
Martin, Beth L., 1957- author.
   Organic wire and metal jewelry : stunning pieces made with sea glass, stones, and crystals / Beth L. Martin, Eva M. Sherman.

   pages : color illustrations ; cm

   Issued also as an ebook.
   ISBN: 978-0-87116-704-0

   1. Wire jewelry—Handbooks, manuals, etc. 2. Metal-work—Handbooks, manuals, etc. 3. Jewelry making—Handbooks, manuals, etc. 4. Found objects (Art)—Handbooks, manuals, etc. I. Sherman, Eva M., author. II. Title.

TT212 .M378 2014
739.274

Contents

Introduction

Sometimes one is lucky enough lucky enough to find a single piece of treasure that is so uniquely beautiful, it needs no other embellishment. Simply hang it on a cord, drape it from a rearview mirror, or wear it on a chain, and allow the wash of sunlight to highlight its natural beauty. Other times, the artistic soul is challenged to add a personal signature to a piece that captures the imagination. These lovely gems, recycled by nature, are transformed and gilded by the individual designer's vision. The settings may be simple, or they may be more complicated, but we are awestruck by the masterful works created by the combination of nature, art, and metal.

As residents of the North Coast with access to Lake Erie, we developed a life-long love affair with glass tumbled and polished by the waves. Designing jewelry incorporating these hidden gems was the natural progression from collector to artist, and the projects developed in this book were a result of incorporating the natural and organic beauty of sea glass into a piece of wearable art. Along the way, we discovered other types of recycled materials with the same organic and raw nature, and we began to use them in our designs.

That's how this book came to be. We recommend experimenting with various beads, crystals, recycled materials, or found objects to create any of the projects found in these pages. Each piece is shown two different ways, so you can see how your own found treasure can be incorporated for a totally unique look. If you're new to wireworking or metal-working, begin with the techniques chapter and beginner projects—we'll take you step by step through each piece, with plenty of photos to guide you as you make your own beautiful creations. If you already have some jewelry-making skills, you'll find plenty of options for creating stunning pieces in the chapters that follow. Enjoy!

— Beth and Eva

Materials

ABOUT WIRE AND METAL SHEET

Buying wire and metal sheet is fairly easy, but it's best to know a little about your choices before you buy. Follow our lead and use the wire, metal, and beads in the materials list, or choose similar ingredients to put your own spin on the designs.

Metals

Wire and sheet is available in a wide range of materials. **Copper** is far-and-away our favorite material to work with because it is soft, affordable, and can be manipulated in many different ways. If you're just starting out, we recommend beginning with copper, which is available in both sheet and wire form. Practice techniques in this metal, and you won't have to worry about making mistakes with the more-expensive material.

Once you've got the hang of working with copper, you'll find that many projects are beautiful when worked in **silver filled, sterling** or **Argentium silver**, or **fine silver**. Fine silver is the purest, composed almost entirely of silver. However, fine silver is fairly soft and can be expensive. It will stay white and lustrous without much polishing, since it oxidizes at a slow rate. It also doesn't have to be pickled after heating.

Sterling silver and **Argentium sterling silver** are perfect for most jewelry-making applications, since they have been alloyed with other metals for additional strength. Sterling silver is strong and malleable; it is 92.5% fine silver with 7.5% copper and other metals. The drawback to sterling is that it tends to tarnish quickly. Argentium sterling is an alloy that substitutes a higher content of germanium to avoid the tarnishing problem while retaining the strength of the metal. Argentium is a bit stiffer than sterling.

Temper

The temper of metal is its hardness, or malleability. Metal can be purchased at different levels of hardness, such as dead-soft, half-hard, or full-hard. When working with metal, you want it to be pliable enough to manipulate, yet strong enough to hold its shape. Working with metal strengthens it; this is called work-hardening. Additional strength comes with hammering after you've formed your shape. When connecting elements with wire-wrapped loops, wrapping the loops is usually enough manipulation to fully work-harden the wire so it is at its maximum strength. Use dead-soft wire for most of the projects in this book.

Silver, gold-filled, and copper wire

wire gauge

Gauge

Sauge is the measure of a sheet or wire's thickness, or diameter. The higher the gauge number, the thinner the metal. Thicker metal is more difficult to work with, while thinner metal has less strength.

Thick metal, such as 12- and 14-gauge, is most appropriate for projects where strength is a necessary element of the design, such as bangle bracelets. For projects and components that need to be strong, but not quite as sturdy or bulky—such as wrapping wire—16- and 18-gauge wire is more appropriate. 20- and 22-gauge wire and sheet is commonly used for most jewelry-making elements, and is perfect for loops and findings. Fine wires are used with small-holed beads, or for decorative elements.

An American-standard wire gauge displays gauges on one side and the corresponding-diameter decimal measurements on the other. A gauge is measured by the width of each slot on the perimeter of the tool, not by the size of the hole.

Wire Shape

Wire comes in a variety of shapes, ranging from the traditional round profile to half-round, flat or square, triangular, and twisted. You can make your own twisted wire by twisting two pieces together.

Findings

Sometimes, instead of making your own metal components, you'll want to finish off a piece of jewelry with findings, such as clasps and earrings wires. To connect those components, you will need to use jump rings (small circles of wire) and headpins (a straight piece of wire with one flat or decorative end to keep beads from sliding off).

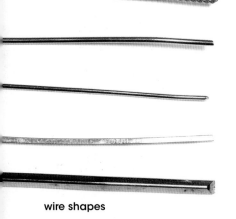

wire shapes

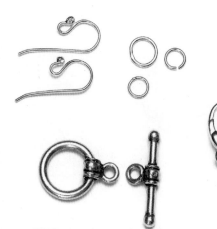

findings

Pearls

These treasures from the sea are the perfect complement for beach stones and sea glass. Since they are each created in water, there is a natural artistic compatibility. Pearls are timeless and elegant, and perfect for casual as well as formal designs.

Glass pearls, such as those created by Swarovski, are an economical substitute for natural pearls.

Sea Glass

Sea glass (also known as beach glass and mermaid tears) is found along large lake and ocean shores. This glass is the ultimate treasure created from trash, as Mother Nature takes broken pieces of glass and upcycles them to small frosted glass gems.

Perhaps you wonder as you walk the beaches where these glass and other shoreline findings began their journey...

Decades ago, glass manufacturing companies needed to be along waterways to produce their product. This also gave them a ready site to dispose of remnants. Other glass may come from shipwrecks and garbage dump sites before it became illegal to dispose of trash in this manner. We affectionately refer to common sea glass colors as Budweiser Brown and Heineken Green.

With literally tens of thousands of glass remnants recycled by the sea, they continually wash up along the shores and are readily available to the artist seeking to create beautiful jewelry.

Gemstones

Semiprecious gemstones are the perfect way to add organic beauty to jewelry designs. There are more than 130 types of stones, minerals, and crystals—such as garnets, aquamarine, citrine, and apatite—to name a few. In most cases, the definition of semi-precious has more to do with the quality of the stone, and less to do with the composition of the mineral that makes up the stone.

Semi-precious stones are often treated using a variety of methods for coloration and stabilization. For example, almost all turquoise has been treated with a transparent resin in order to stabilize it, as it is a fragile and porous stone in an untreated state. Many other stones are either heat-treated or irradiated to enhance their colors. Nearly all can be fashioned into beads or pendants for creating jewelry.

Natural stones that have been drilled, such as turquoise, make an excellent component for organic jewelry designs.

Crystals

Crystals are man-made gems. Swarovski Crystals are the industry standard and are manufactured in Austria. In the late 1800's, Daniel Swarovski discovered a formula for making beautiful, high-quality lead glass crystals. Since then, the Swarovski family has continued the tradition of making the most recognized crystals in the world out of their factory in Wattens, a market community in Austria.

These sparkly goodies come in various shapes, sizes, and colors. For these projects, we were inspired by the traditional bicone and faceted round crystals, but you can always use whatever shade and shape you desire.

Tools

There are a few essential tools, but there are limitless numbers of optional tools. It is best to do some research and find the equipment that matches your budget and needs.

WIREWORKING TOOLS

Pliers are essential tools for most wireworking tasks. When purchasing pliers, inspect the jaws to see that they are smooth and even, look for a sold joint with little give or wiggle, and try the handles for comfort. Listed below are some basic types of pliers and their functions:

Chainnose pliers have flat inner jaws and a pointed end, and they are suitable for gripping and shaping wire. These pliers can also be used for opening and closing jump rings or other loops.

Flatnose pliers are similar to chainnose pliers, but they have a flattened end, making it easier to create sharper bends in the wire.

Nylon-jaw pliers have replaceable nylon linings on the jaws, which protect the wire from tool marks. These pliers are useful for straightening wire.

Roundnose pliers are critical for making loops and bends. These pliers have conical jaws, which are perfect for shaping wire loops.

Bail-making pliers are handy for creating loops of a specific size.

Wire cutters produce a flat cut on one of the wire ends. Side cutters are the most common type of cutter. Their blades are parallel to the handles and are useful for cutting wire from any angle.

An **awl** is used to nudge wire ends into place.

You'll also need a flexible **measuring tape**.

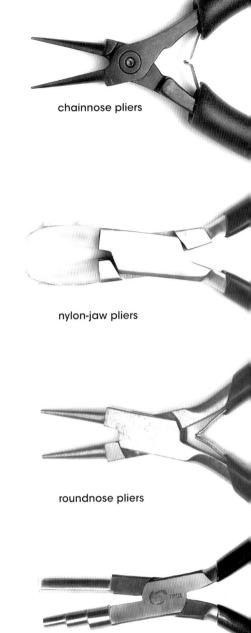

chainnose pliers

nylon-jaw pliers

roundnose pliers

bail-making pliers

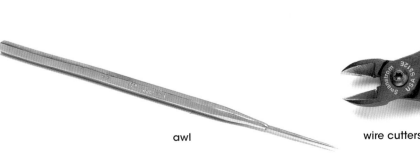

awl

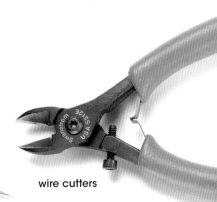

wire cutters

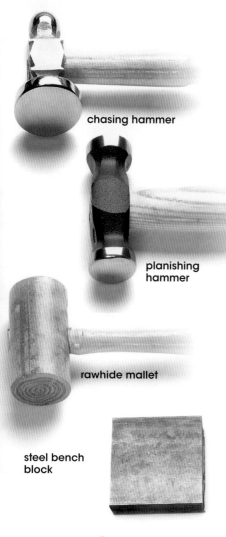

chasing hammer

planishing hammer

rawhide mallet

steel bench block

dapping set

ring mandrel

METALWORKING TOOLS

There is a wide variety of jewelry-making hammers available and each has a specific purpose.

Household hammers are used for striking against other tools, such as stamps and disk cutters. Do not use any other hammer for this purpose. If the surface of a jewelry hammer becomes marred due to misuse, the mars will transfer to the metal.

Chasing hammers are a modified version of the ball-peen hammer, and they can be used to apply texture, rivet, or compress metal.

Planishing hammers have two flat, rounded faces and can be used to smooth and flatten the surface of the metal.

Texture hammers have engravings on the face and are used to apply texture to the metal.

Nylon, **rubber**, and **rawhide mallets** are used to shape and form metal without leaving marks and scratches.

A **steel bench block** provides a hard, smooth surface on which to stamp or planish your pieces.

A **dapping** or **doming block** is a steel block with a series of concave circles on its surfaces. Use a household hammer with the **dapping punches** to form the metal pieces into the indentations.

Mandrels are made of steel, plastic, or wood, and have a smooth or stepped taper for measuring rings and bracelets. You can use unconventional mandrels that fit any size or shape you like. We use piano wire mandrels for coiling wire (which can be found online or at some hobby shops).

Rotary drills, such as Dremels, are used for drilling holes in glass and stone surfaces. Typically, we use a hollow-core diamond drill bit with a fitted collet. A flex shaft attached to the drill allows for more control of the drill.

We like to use a **cordless drill** in conjunction with a **piano wire mandrel** to create coiled wire.

A **stamp** is a metal tool used for making an impression on metal surfaces. The stamp is held above the metal's surface, then struck with a household hammer, forcing it into the metal and leaving an impression on the surface. For clean, clear stamping, always place the metal to be stamped on a steel bench block before striking.

rotary drill

disk cutter

solder brick

Use a **metal hole punch** for making holes in sheet metal. The standard size used in this book is 1.5mm.

Disk cutters are used to cut perfect circles from metal. If you don't have a disk cutter, you can substitute purchased disk blanks.

Metal shears are used to cut sheet metal. Joyce Chen kitchen scissors were used for the majority of the projects in this book. They easily cut up to 20-gauge metal.

Metal files are used to refine and shape the edges of sheet metal and wire surfaces. Sanding blocks or emery boards are used to smooth any remaining roughness.

TORCHES AND HOT TOOLS
CAUTION: When using a torch, pickle, or liver of sulfur, always work in a well-ventilated area.

Torches are necessary for annealing metal, brazing wire, and balling wire ends. For the projects in this book, we used the Bernzo-matic Torch with MAPP gas. You can substitute a butane torch or other torch of your choice. Be sure to read and follow all of the manufacturer's instructions carefully.

Solder bricks or **charcoal blocks** are fire-resistant and absorb heat. Protect your work surface by placing a ceramic tile underneath the solder brick, and ALWAYS work in a well-ventilated area.

Cross-locking tweezers are used to pick up hot wire and metal. Quench hot metal in a ceramic or glass bowl of water.

Pickle is a mild acid used to clean firescale from metal. Using a dedicated **crock pot**, fill the crock pot ⅔ with water and add one tablespoon of pickle per two cups of water. Pickle is also sold generically as Sparex or pH Down. ALWAYS use copper tongs with pickle, as stainless steel tongs will cause copper plating of metals in the pickle. Take care to keep the pickle off clothing and skin.

FINISHING TOOLS
Use a **brass brush** to polish metal pieces after removing them from the pickle.

Tumblers with stainless steel shot and burnishing compounds are used to polish and shine metal pieces. Typically, you'll want to tumble a finished piece for 3–12 hours.

Using **liver of sulfur** adds a dark, antiqued look (or patina) to a finished piece. Polishing with an abrasive **polishing pad** highlights the metal.

We recommend sealing copper for two reasons: It tarnishes rather quickly, and some people react to bare copper on skin. Our pieces have been sealed with a **spray gloss sealer** that is designed for metal.

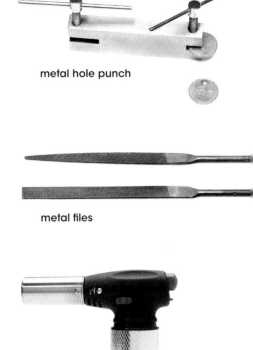
metal hole punch

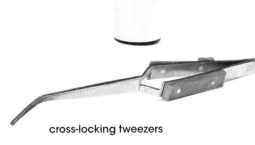
metal files

torch

cross-locking tweezers

stamp set

rotary tumbler

Basics

Drilling Glass and Stone

Learning to drill is one of the foundational techniques for creating jewelry with found natural objects, such as sea glass or river stones. Use the instructions below whenever the projects in the following chapters require drilled focals.

practice material

object to be drilled

Note: Before drilling, thoroughly clean the object in hot water with a small amount of bleach to kill any bacteria. This is especially important if the piece is a found object.

toolkit

Pencil

Plastic tray

Small piece of wood to fit inside plastic tray

Sponge

Dremel or rotary drill (to use the drill, follow the manufacturer's instructions)

Hollow-core diamond drill bit (1–2.5mm x 1½ in. long)

Collet to fit drill bit

Linseed oil (optional)

Chainnose pliers or a craft stick

Safety glasses (recommended)

Ear protectors (recommended)

Flex shaft attachment (recommended)

Step 1 Mark the spot to be drilled on the front of your object with a pencil. In a plastic tray, place the piece of wood first, then the sponge, and then the object to be drilled. Fill the tray with water so the object is immersed to prevent the object and/or drill bit from breaking. Fit the drill bit into the collet before placing it inside the chuck, and tighten. Set the drill to medium high to high: 30,000–35,000 rpm.

Step 2 (a) Dip the drill bit in linseed oil (optional).

(b) Hold the drill bit above the object at a 45-degree angle.

(c) Begin drilling, and immediately straighten the drill. **Tip: To hold the object in place, use a pair of pliers or a craft stick.**

Step 3 Drill straight down into the object. Stop every few seconds and dip the drill bit into linseed oil to keep the drill bit cool, and keep the object submerged underwater while drilling. Drill halfway through the object, turn the piece over, and drill from the opposite side. **Tip: When drilling sea glass, turn the piece over and find the white dot—this is silica buildup. Use the white dot as a guide to drill from the opposite side.**

Step 4 When you have finished drilling the hole, rinse and wipe dry.

Step 5 Follow Steps 1–4 to drill other shoreline findings, such as pottery, river stones, china pieces, clay brick, and even fossils. We recommend that you don't drill shells, as breathing the particles may be toxic.

How To: Setting a Grommet

A silver grommet makes a beautiful setting. For an elegant touch, add grommets to your drilled glass or stone.

practice materials

object to be drilled

2 5mm silver grommets

toolkit

Drilling Glass and Stone toolkit, p. 12

Hollow-core diamond drill bit (5mm x 1.5 in. long)

Center punch

Household hammer

Jewelers glue (optional)

Step 1 Following Steps 1–2c of Drilling Glass and Stone, drill a partial hole in the object. This pilot hole helps prevent any cracking or chipping of the glass or stone.

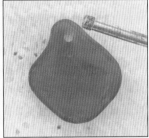

Step 2 (a) Replace the drill bit with a 5mm hollow-core diamond drill bit.

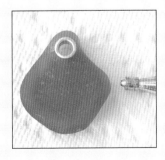

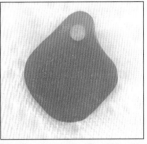

(b) Drill into the partial hole with the 5mm drill bit. Turn the object over, and repeat Steps 1 and 2a on the opposite side.

Step 3 Gently tap the grommet into the object with a center punch and a household hammer, making sure that it is tight and secure. Repeat on the opposite side, spreading the end to hold the grommet in place. Use a tiny drop of jewelers glue if needed.

Creating a Wire-Wrapped Loop

Use this technique to create loops and bails to secure dangles and drops.

practice materials
6 in. 18-, 20-, 22-, or
  24-gauge copper wire

toolkit
Roundnose pliers
Chainnose pliers
Wire cutters

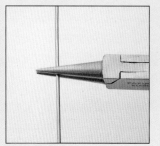

Step 1 With your non-dominant hand, grasp the piece of wire vertically with roundnose pliers 3 in. from the top. The roundnose pliers will be horizontal. **Tip: For a small loop, grasp the wire close to the tip of the roundnose pliers. For a large loop, grasp the wire near the pliers' handles.**

Step 2 Bend the wire end over the top of the pliers' jaws 90 degrees. **Tip: Use your fingers, or grip the wire end with the chainnose pliers.**

Step 3 Reposition the pliers to grasp the top of the bend. The pliers will now be vertical.

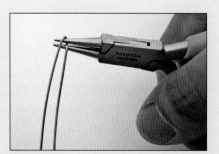

Step 4 Bring the wire end up and around the top jaws until it is pointing straight down.

Step 5 Adjust your grip again, moving the pliers to a horizontal position. Wrap the wire until it sits at a 90-degree angle from the original vertical wire. You have now created a full loop. If you are going to attach the loop to another link or loop, do it now, before adding the wraps.

Tip: To open a plain loop or jump ring, hold the loop with two pairs of chainnose or flatnose pliers, one on each side, and push one forward and the other back, to open. Never pull the loop from side to side, or you'll pull it out of shape. Reverse these movements to close the loop.

Step 6 Holding the loop firmly with chainnose pliers, wrap the wire end around the vertical wire a few times, making the wraps neat and parallel. Trim the excess wire. **Tip: You can make wire-wrapped loops with multiple pieces of wire**—simply hold the wires as one bundle while following Steps 1–6.

 # Creating a Flat Spiral

In many projects, you'll be directed to finish wire ends with a decorative flat spiral. Make these spirals as large or as small as you like, depending on the length of wire used.

practice materials
6 in. 18-gauge wire

toolkit
Roundnose pliers
Chainnose pliers
Wire cutters
Chasing hammer (optional)
Steel bench block (optional)

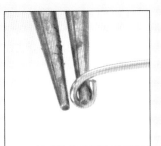

Step 1 (a) Hold the end of a wire with the very tip of your roundnose pliers. Slowly rotate the pliers, pulling the wire in a circular motion.

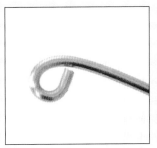

(b) Stop when you've formed a small loop.

Step 2 Grasp the loop with chainnose pliers. Continue rolling the spiral until you reach the desired size.

Step 3 Trim the wire as desired. **Tip: Hammer the spiral with a chasing hammer on a steel block. This is called work-hardening, and it gives metal added strength.**

How To: Coiling Wire

Rather than wrapping small-gauge wire by hand, use a drill to speed up the process and ensure nice, even coils.

practice materials

24-gauge or lighter wire (use directly from spool)

toolkit

12-in. 20-gauge piano wire mandrel

Wire cutters

Variable speed drill

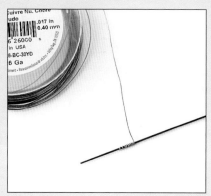

Step 1 Wrap the wire end around the end of the piano wire mandrel 7–8 times to anchor, and trim any excess wire.

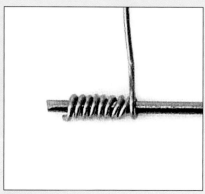

Step 2 Push the coils together.

Step 3 Insert the coiled wire and the mandrel into the chuck, and tighten. Make sure the chuck grabs some of the coiled wire, or only the mandrel will spin.

Step 4 Brace the mandrel with your index finger, and guide the wire with your thumb and middle finger. Begin coiling the wire at a slow speed. **Tip: Be careful not to put too much tension on the wire, or it will be difficult to remove the coil from the mandrel later.**

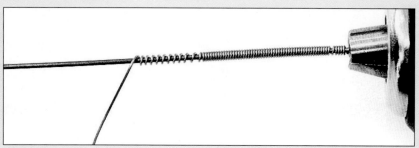

Step 5 (a) If the wires spread apart, compress the coil before removing it from the mandrel.

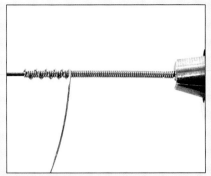

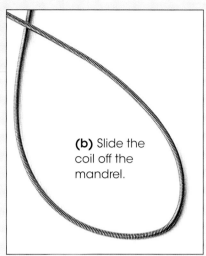

(b) If the wire coils back on itself, stop the drill, reverse, and unwind to where the mistake began. Reset the drill to a forward motion, and continue coiling.

Step 6 (a) Stop coiling when you reach the end of the mandrel. Remove the mandrel from the chuck, trim the excess wire, and compress the coils together.

(b) Slide the coil off the mandrel.

How To: Annealing

To anneal metal means to heat it to a specific temperature so it's pliable and easy to work with. Firescale is a dirty-looking, black substance that appears on metal after annealing. You will need to remove it before completing a project.

practice materials

1x6 in. sheet metal

toolkit

Safety glasses

Solder brick

Ceramic tile

Torch

Cross-locking tweezers

Glass or ceramic bowl filled with water

Crock pot

Lump-form pickle

Copper tongs

Brass brush

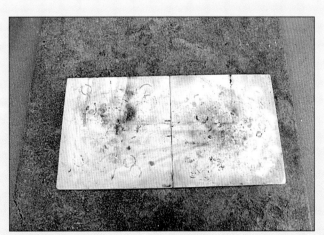

Step 1
Choose a sturdy, flat surface for working. Gather your materials and tools so they are all close at hand. Place the solder brick on the ceramic tile. Create a pickle solution (see Step 4). **Tip: Ceramic tile will protect your work surface from the heat of the flame.** Let the solder brick cool between annealings to avoid cracking the tile.

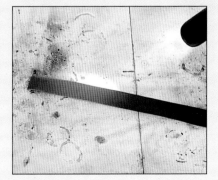

CAUTION: Be very careful when working with gas and flame. Read the manufacturer's instructions for your torch carefully, and wear safety glasses at all times.

Step 2 Place the metal sheet on the solder brick. Turn on your torch, following manufacturer's instructions. Heat the metal until it glows dull red. Don't heat the metal to a cherry red; when it is heated to a dull red, it is annealed. Turn off the torch.

Step 3 (a) Pick up the metal with cross-locking tweezers and quench in a water-filled bowl.

(b) The metal will remain annealed even after it has cooled. **Tip: To avoid rusting tools, make sure the metal has been dried thoroughly.**

Step 4 Place the metal in a pickle solution. To create the solution: Fill a crock pot ⅔ full of water, and add 1½ tablespoons of lump-form pickle. Let the water heat up. When ready, place the annealed metal in the crock pot for about 10 minutes. Use only copper tongs to insert and remove the metal, in order to avoid contaminating the pickle. **Tip: Pickle emits fumes, so work in a well-ventilated area. When the pickle solution turns swimming pool blue, it is saturated and time to change the solution. It is very important to neutralize the pickle before it can be disposed safely. Neutralize the pickle in a large container by adding small amounts of baking soda until it stops bubbling. When the bubbling has stopped, it is safe to dispose of the solution.**

Step 5 Remove the metal from the pickle solution. Rinse and dry.

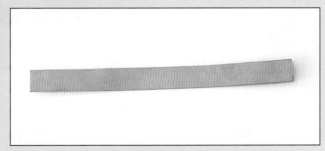

Step 6 (a) Polish the metal with a stiff brass brush to remove any remaining firescale.

(b) The metal is now ready to be textured or forged. **Tip: Tumbling for a few hours in a tumbler filled with stainless steel shot will also polish the metal (see p. 23).**

⟨How To:⟩ Balling Wire Ends

A balled wire end gives a professional-looking touch to a piece, and it's very easy to do. You can use this technique with just about any size wire; it's perfect for creating decorative ball-end headpins as well.

practice material
3 in. 18-, 20-, 22-, or 24-gauge wire

toolkit
Annealing toolkit, p. 17
Bench vise

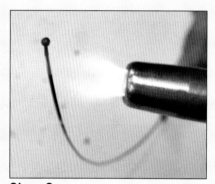

Step 1 Prepare your work space as in Annealing, p. 17, except secure the torch to your work surface with a bench vise so it stands facing away from you vertically. Turn on the torch. Pick up a piece of wire with cross-locking tweezers at the bottom, and hold it vertically. Holding the wire vertically will cause the wire to form a nice, centered ball.

Step 2 Raise the top wire end into the hottest part of the flame. **Tip: The hottest part of the flame is approximately 2 in. away from the tip of the torch.** When the end of the wire glows cherry red, a ball will begin to form. **Tip: The process will only take a few seconds.**

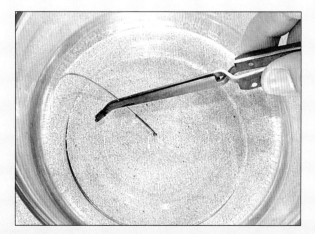

Step 3 When the ball is the desired size, remove the wire from the flame and immediately quench in a bowl of water. Pickle, if desired.

How To: Brazing Copper

Use this simple and secure method for connecting copper wires to capture a stone or piece of glass. (This method works for copper only.)

practice materials
2 6-in. 18, 20, 22 or 24-gauge copper wires

Brazing rod (found online or at many home improvement stores)

toolkit
Annealing toolkit, p. 17

Step 1 Prepare your workspace as in Annealing, p. 17. Place the wires on your block so they are touching.

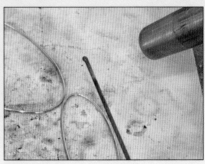

Step 2 Holding the brazing rods with cross-locking tweezers, heat the wires and brazing rods with the torch.

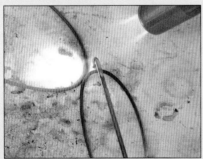

Step 3
Touch the melting brazing rod to the two wires.

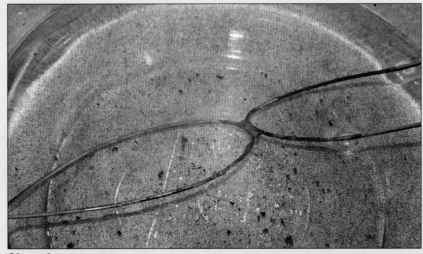

Step 4 Quench.

How To: Forging Metal

Forging is the process of shaping metal using heat and compressive force. You can forge a ring, a cuff, a curved pin, a necklace component, or any metal shape.

practice materials

18-, 20-, 22- or 24-gauge sheet metal

toolkit

Annealing toolkit, p. 17

Rubber mallet

Bracelet mandrel

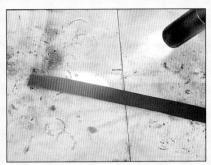

Step 1 Prepare your workspace and anneal the metal (see p. 17). **Tip: Softening the metal makes it easier to manipulate and shape during forging.**

Step 2 Bend the metal sheet around a mandrel, and hammer with a rubber mallet to work-harden. **Tip: Using a rubber mallet keeps the metal from picking up dings and other marks.**

How To: Texturing Metal

Textured sheet metal can add interest to a piece. Construct a careful pattern, or hammer randomly for a freeform design.

practice material

18-, 20-, 22- or 24-gauge sheet metal

toolkit

Annealing toolkit, p. 17

Texture hammer

Steel block

Step 1 Prepare your workspace and anneal the metal sheet (see p. 17).

Step 2 Hammer the metal with a texture hammer. Use firm, consistent strokes for even texture. **Tip: The metal is now work-hardened. Anneal, if required, to continue shaping the metal into the desired form. Applying liver of sulfur patina and polishing (see p. 23) brings out texture.**

How To: Stamping Metal

For a personal touch, add a decorative stamp to your piece. You could also use this technique for creating your own custom textured sheet, if desired—just be sure to anneal the sheet afterward if you plan to form it.

practice materials

18- or 20-gauge sheet metal

toolkit

Steel block

Metal stamp

Household hammer

Finishing toolkit (optional)

Step 1 Place the metal sheet on the steel block. Position a metal stamp vertically at the desired location.

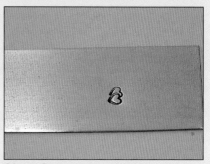

Step 2 Apply a solid blow at exactly 90 degrees with the household hammer to the metal stamp to imprint the metal. Don't tap lightly or multiple times in the same spot, or you'll create a blurry imprint. **Tip: Applying liver of sulfur patina and polishing (see p. 23) brings out the texture of the stamp.**

How To: Riveting

Connect two pieces of metal together with this simple, secure method.

practice materials

2 1x2 in. 18-, 20-, 22-, 24-, or 26-gauge sheet metal pieces

½-in. 1.3mm-diameter nailhead rivet

toolkit

Permanent marker

1.5mm metal hole punch

Metal file

Steel block or mandrel

Wire cutters

Chasing hammer

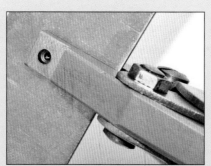

Step 1 Layer two pieces of sheet metal, and mark the desired connection location with a permanent marker on the top sheet. Remove the bottom sheet, and punch a hole in the top sheet. If there is a burr, file it smooth. **Tip: Most files will only cut when you are moving the file away from you.**

Step 2 Layer the two sheets again. Punch through the second layer, using the top hole as a pilot hole. Most metal hole punches will punch thicknesses up to 20-gauge. If the metal is thicker, you'll need to use a drill.

   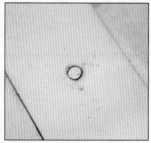

Step 3 Insert the nailhead rivet into both holes, from bottom to top. Lay the sheets-and-rivet sandwich on the steel block. Trim the rivet so 1⁄16 in. of the rivet remains above the top sheet (approximately the thickness of a credit card).

Step 4 Hammer the rivet with the ball end of the chasing hammer until the top of the nailhead rivet is totally flush with the metal sheet. As you hammer, the metal spreads to cover the hole. Run your finger over the front and back of the rivet to make sure both sides are flush. If they are not flush, keep hammering.

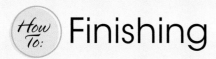

Finishing

When you've finished constructing your piece, consider tumble-polishing and adding patina. Patina gives an "antique" look to copper or silver.

practice materials

Finished metal piece

toolkit

Rotary tumbler and steel shot

Dishwashing liquid or burnishing compound

Liver of sulfur solution

Bowl of cold water

Fine steel wool

Polishing cloth

Step 1
Tumble the piece in a rotary tumbler with steel shot, if desired. Tumble for 2–3 hours.

Step 2
Clean the piece thoroughly with soapy water. Prepare a liver of sulfur (LOS) solution according to the manufacturer's instructions. **Tip: We prefer to use lump-form LOS, which dissolves in warm water.** Dip the piece in the LOS solution, and watch as it changes color. When you have the color you want, remove the piece from the LOS solution and rinse in clean water.

Step 3
Brush the piece with fine steel wool to remove some of the patina, if desired. Use a polishing cloth to remove even more patina.

Beginner
projects

Waterspout
earrings

Looking for drama? Try using
this coiled wire technique to
create fabulous earrings! Flashy
pink crystals against a silver swirl
backdrop are guaranteed to
be eye-catching, and a pair
made from blue sea glass drops
accented with matching crystals
is equally breathtaking.

materials

PINK CRYSTAL EARRINGS

2 15mm top-drilled (front-to-back) pear-shaped pink crystal briolettes

6 4mm pink bicone crystals

40 in. 20-gauge half-hard silver wire

6 1-in. silver headpins

2 10mm silver jump rings

2 8mm silver jump rings

Pair of silver earring wires

BLUE GLASS EARRINGS

2 15mm top-drilled pear-shaped blue sea glass nuggets (see p. 12)

6 4mm blue bicone crystals

40 in. 20-gauge half-hard silver wire

6 1-in. silver headpins

2 15mm silver jump rings

2 8mm silver jump rings

Pair of silver earring wires

tools

Tape measure

Chainnose pliers

Wire cutters

Roundnose pliers

Center-drilled wood dowel (½-in. diameter x 1¾-in. long with a 1mm center-drilled hole)

Chasing hammer

Step 1

String a crystal briolette on each 10mm jump ring, or string a sea glass nugget on each 15mm jump ring. String a 4mm crystal on each 1-in. headpin, and make wire-wrapped loops above the crystals to create crystal dangles (see p. 14). String three 4mm crystal dangles on a 8mm jump ring, and repeat with the remaining three dangles and 8mm jump ring. Tip: You may need larger or smaller jump rings to fit the holes in your briolettes.

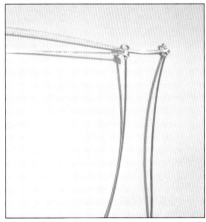

Step 2

Cut the 20-gauge wire into two 20-in. pieces. Approximately one-third of the way from the bottom of each wire, make a small wire-wrapped loop. The shorter end is the vertical end.

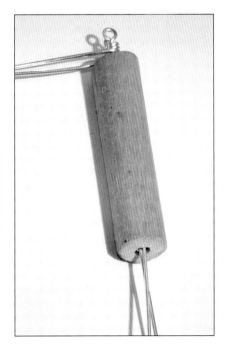

Step 3

Place the short ends of both wires in the center-drilled hole of the wood dowel.

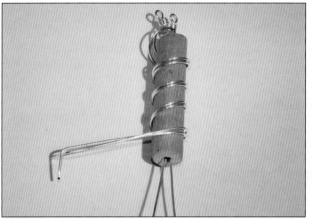

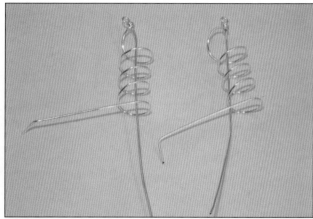

Step 4

Keeping the long wires parallel, wrap the wires around the wood dowel in a spiral motion, leaving about 2 in. straight at the end. Work-harden the wires on the dowel by tapping them gently with the flat end of the chasing hammer.

Step 5

Remove the wires from the wood dowel, and unwind carefully to separate them.

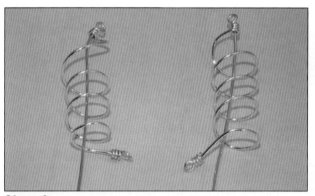

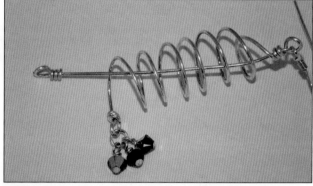

Step 6

(a) At the end of each coiled wire, make a small wire-wrapped loop.

(b) Attach three crystal dangles with an 8mm jump ring to one small wire-wrapped loop. Repeat with the second component and second wire.

Step 7

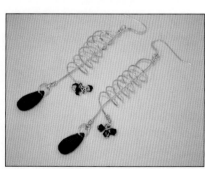

Measuring ¼ in. below the end of the spiral, make a wire-wrapped loop on both wires and attach the briolette or sea glass jump ring component. Attach an earring wire at the top wire-wrapped loop of each component.

Creating both earring spirals at the same time ensures that they will be identical. For a truly organic look, you can spiral each wire separately.

Low Tide
ring

The unexpected juxtaposition of beads, metal, and rubber makes for a totally unique and completely fun ring. Use any bead you like as a centerpiece, whether it's a sea glass nugget or a crystal-studded round. The comfortable rubber band allows for lots of flexibility—and style.

materials

SEA GLASS RING

12mm center-drilled sea glass nugget (see p. 12)

4 16mm cornflake beads

1-in. barbell body piercing component

4x½ in. black neoprene strip

Note: The center hole of the nugget and cornflake beads must fit over the barbell component—approximately 2mm in diameter

CRYSTAL RING

8mm crystal-studded black round bead

6 6mm cornflake beads

1-in. barbell body piercing component

4x½ in. black neoprene strip

tools

Ring mandrel

Tape measure

Scissors

Permanent marker

Awl

Step 1

(a) Center the neoprene on the ring mandrel at the desired ring size.

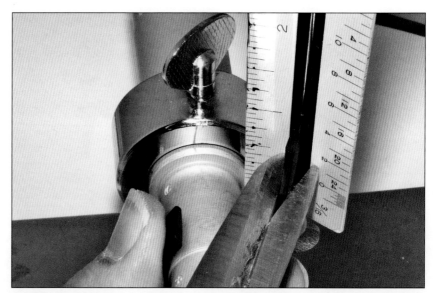

(b) Trim the neoprene with scissors so it projects ½ in. above the top of the ring mandrel on each side.

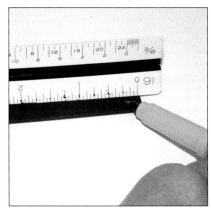

Step 2

Mark each end of the neoprene with a permanent marker ¼ in. away from the ends and centered from side to side.

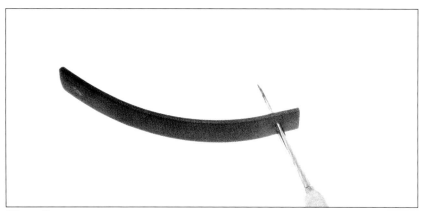

Step 3

Punch a hole with the awl at each mark.

Step 4

Trim both ends of the neoprene with scissors. Round the ends to mimic the shape of the cornflake beads, if desired, or leave them square.

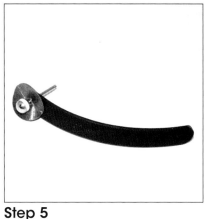

Step 5

(a) Unscrew one end of the barbell component. Begin to stack the components. For the Sea Glass Ring, stack a 12mm cornflake, one end of the neoprene, a 12mm, the sea glass nugget, a 12mm, the other end of the neoprene, and a 12mm. For the Crystal Ring, stack a 6mm cornflake, one end of the neoprene, two 6mms, a crystal-studded round bead, two 6mms, the other end of the neoprene, and a cornflake.

(b) Screw the other end of the barbell to the opposite end.

Pirate's Treasure
pendant and earrings

Create this treasure, and you'll attract pirates on both land and sea! In this project, you'll dangle crystals and pearls from either a glass nugget or a recycled glass ring. String the finished pendant on a simple neck wire, or find a fancy chain for even more shine.

materials

GLASS NUGGET PENDANT

25–30x30–40mm top-drilled (front-to-back) sea glass focal (see p. 12)

6mm white glass pearl

6 4mm white and blue crystals

5 4mm white glass pearls

12 3mm blue crystals

24 2mm silver spacer beads

24 1-in. silver headpins

6mm silver jump ring

1 in. 3mm silver chain

6 in. 20-gauge silver wire

RECYCLED GLASS RING PENDANT

40mm blue recycled glass ring focal

6mm white glass pearl

6 4mm white and blue crystals

5 4mm glass pearls

12 3mm pink and blue crystals

24 2mm silver spacer beads

24 1-in. silver headpins

6mm silver jump ring

1 in. 3mm chain

18 in. fancy silver box chain

6 in. 20-gauge silver wire

GLASS NUGGET EARRINGS

2 10–12x15–20mm top-drilled sea glass focals

2 6mm white glass pearls

8 4mm clear and blue crystals

4 4mm glass pearls

12 3mm crystals

26 2mm spacer beads

26 1-in. headpins

2 ½-in. lengths of 2mm silver chain

2 6-in. lengths of 20-gauge silver wire

2 6mm silver jump rings

Pair of silver earring wires

RECYCLED GLASS RING EARRINGS

2 20–30mm blue recycled glass ring focals

2 6mm white glass pearls

8 4mm white, blue, and clear crystals

2 4mm white glass pearls

12 3mm crystals

26 2mm spacer beads

26 1-in. silver headpins

2 ½-in. lengths of 2mm silver chain

2 6-in. lengths of 20-gauge silver wire

Pair of silver earring wires

2 6mm silver jump rings

tools

Roundnose pliers

Wire cutters

Chainnose pliers

PENDANT
Step 1

For the Glass Nugget Pendant, string the chain and sea glass on the 6-in. wire; for the Recycled Glass Ring Pendant, wrap the wire around the recycled glass ring once on each side of the chain. End with two wires at the top of the focal piece.

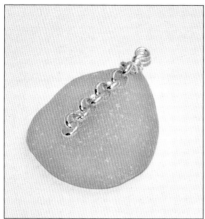

Step 2

Make a wire-wrapped loop, holding both wires as one (see p. 14). Orient the loop parallel to the bead.

Step 3

Create accent bead dangles: String a 2mm spacer bead and a 6mm pearl on a headpin. Make the first half of a wire-wrapped loop. Before finishing the wraps, insert a link of chain in the loop. Close the loop.

Step 4

Repeat Step 3 to attach the accent beads to the chain as desired, varying the color and size of the remaining crystals and pearls, until all pearls and crystals are attached to the chain.

Step 5

Attach a jump ring to the wire-wrapped loop at the top, and slide the pendant on a chain of your choice. Tip: If desired, attach a short length of fancy chain to cover the wraps at the top of the focal before closing the jump ring.

EARRINGS

Repeat Steps 1–4 of the pendant instructions but substitute smaller focals, fewer beads, and shorter lengths of chain as noted in the materials list. Attach each finished component to an earring wire with a jump ring, and attach short lengths of fancy chain, if desired.

The combination of natural and man-made materials is simply stunning.

Waterway
pendant

This sizable piece is embellished with twinkling crystals and spacers for subtle sparkle. Cover most of the surface of your focal piece, as in the stone cabochon example, or let the wraps act as an elegant accent to the main event, as in the sea glass version.

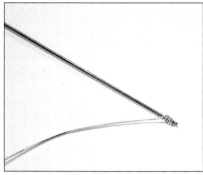

Step 1

Create two 8-in. long coils with 24-gauge wire (see p. 16). Wrap the end of the 20-gauge wire on the mandrel.

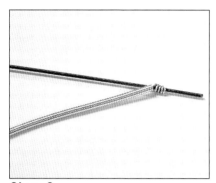

Step 2

(a) Wrap a few coils of the 20-gauge wire onto the mandrel and slide to the end. Slide the coiled wire onto the 20-gauge wire.

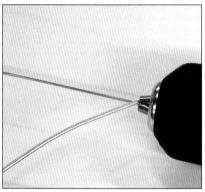

(b) Push the coiled wire up to the mandrel.

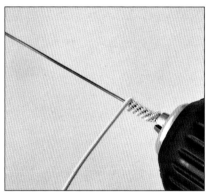

(c) Hold the opposite end of the coiled wire in place to prevent it from sliding back, and slowly begin coiling the coiled wire. Remove the coil from the mandrel, and trim the ends. Repeat with the second coil.

materials

SEA GLASS PENDANT

25x35mm (approx.) sea glass nugget focal, undrilled

18 3mm blue bicone crystals

19 2mm silver spacer beads

4 ft. 20-gauge silver wire

4 ft. 22-gauge silver wire

12 ft. 24-gauge silver wire

GEMSTONE PENDANT

25x35mm (approx.) stone cabochon focal

19 4mm purple bicone crystals

30 copper spacer beads or 11º seed beads

4 ft. 20-gauge copper wire

4 ft. 22-gauge copper wire

12 ft. 24-gauge copper wire

Note: The spacer beads and bicone crystals must fit over the 22-gauge wire.

tools

Coiling Wire toolkit, p. 16

Tape measure

Wire cutter

Roundnose pliers

Finishing toolkit, p. 23 (optional)

Step 3

String the first coiled wire on the 22-gauge wire, string a bicone crystal, and then string the second coiled wire. Center the coils on the 22-gauge wire.

Step 4

Wrap the coils around the sea glass nugget or stone cabochon focal.

Step 5

Bend the coils around the focal, following its shape, until you reach the top. Remove the focal.

Step 6

Trim the coils so they meet at the top of the shape. **Tip: Be careful not to cut the 22-gauge wire.**

Step 7

Make a wire-wrapped loop, holding both 22-gauge wires as one (see p. 14). Trim the excess wire.

Step 8

Fit the focal into your newly formed coiled bezel.

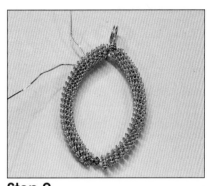

Step 9

Cut 20 in. of 22-gauge wire, and anchor one end to the coiled bezel by wrapping between the coils a few times. Trim and tuck the excess wire.

Tip: The number of times the wire will cross the front and back of the focal depends on the size and shape of the focal. Wrap a minimum of three times for stability.

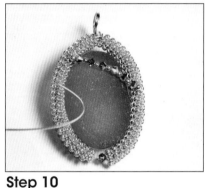

Step 10

(a) String alternating spacer beads and bicone crystals to cover a straight line across the front of the focal. Cross the focal at a bit of an angle.

(b) Wrap the crystal-and-spacer-embellished wire between a coil on one side of the piece, across the back, and between a coil on the other side of the piece. Repeat Step 10 as desired, keeping the wraps parallel.

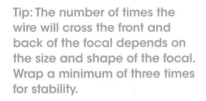

Step 11

When you have the desired number of wraps around the focal, anchor the wire end by wrapping it between the coils a few times. Trim and tuck any excess wire.

Step 12

Snug up the wires wraps by gently twisting the wraps on the back of the piece with the tip of your roundnose pliers. Tumble-polish and add patina as desired (see p. 23).

Gifts from the Sea
earrings

Wrap it up! Put a bow on it! We promise you will love these gifts from the sea featuring surf-tumbled glass polished by Mother Nature herself. Create a petite version with a square glass bead or make a statement with large oval sea glass nuggets.

materials

OVAL NUGGET EARRINGS

2 15x20mm oval sea glass nugget, undrilled

27 in. 20-gauge square half-hard silver wire

12 in. 18-gauge half-round silver wire

2 6mm silver jump rings

Pair of silver earring wires

SQUARE BEAD EARRINGS

2 10mm square beads

18 in. 20-gauge square half-hard silver wire

12 in. 18-gauge half-round silver wire

2 6mm silver jump rings

Pair of silver earring wires

tools

Nylon-jaw pliers

Tape measure

Permanent marker

Painters tape

Wire cutters

Chainnose pliers

Roundnose pliers

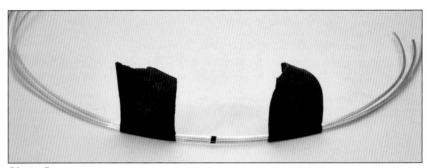

Step 1

Cut the 20-gauge wire into 9-in. pieces. Cut two pieces for the Square Bead Earrings, and cut three pieces for the Oval Nugget Earrings. Straighten the wires with nylon-jaw pliers, and mark the centerpoint of the wires with a permanent marker. Bundle the wires together and place painter's tape on both sides of the centerpoint, keeping the wires parallel.

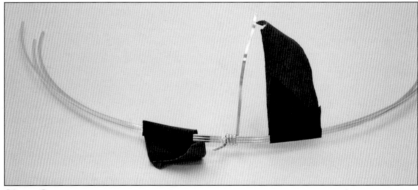

Step 2

Cut two 6-in. lengths of 18-gauge half-round wire. Bind one 6-in. length of half-round wire around the two (or three) strands of square wire at the centerpoint. Use nylon-jaw pliers to compress the half-round wire after each wrap.

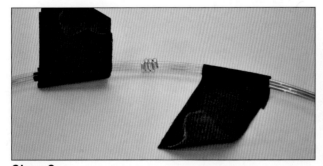

Step 3

Trim the half-round wire, and carefully tuck the wire end inside the wraps.

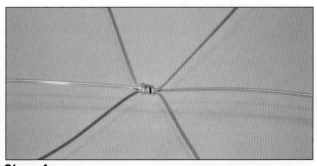

Step 4

Remove the painter's tape. For the Oval Nugget Earrings, use chainnose pliers to create a star shape by bending two wires up and two wires down as shown. For the Square Bead Earrings, bend one wire up and one wire down to form a cross.

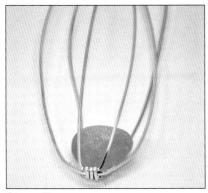

Step 5
Insert the oval nugget or square bead, and bend the wires up to form a cage.

Step 6
Bend two wires up from opposite sides. Use chainnose pliers to create a 90-degree bend, so the wires meet at the top and form an L. Tape the wires together.

Step 7
Repeat Step 6 with the remaining two or four wires.

Step 8
Pull all of the wires together and bind with the remaining 6-in. length of half-round wire. Trim the excess half-round wire. (For the Square Bead Earrings, skip Steps 8 and 9 and make a wrapped loop with two parallel lengths of square wire.)

Step 9
(a) For the Oval Nugget Earrings, remove the painter's tape. Bend all but one of the wires away from the nugget.

(b) Using the center wire, make a wire-wrapped loop (see p. 14).

Step 10
Trim the remaining square wires to 1½ in. Create flat spirals with the wire ends (see p. 15), and place as desired. Attach an earring wire to the wire-wrapped loop using a 6mm jump ring.

Step 11
Repeat Steps 1–10 to make a second earring.

Entangled
pendant

Capture an irregular triangle shape
with this simply wrapped project. Warm
copper sets off either a cool piece of
sea glass or a translucent gemstone
nugget. Embellish with spirals at the top
or make a messy wrap to finish off this
easy-but-elegant piece.

Step 1
Cut the 20-gauge wire into three 2-ft. pieces. Hold the three wires parallel, and find the center. With bail-making pliers, make a wire-wrapped loop (p. 14), using all three wires to make the wraps.

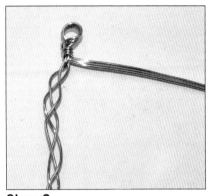

Step 2
Loosely braid the vertical wires. You want a carefree, organic look, so don't make the braids too uniform.

materials

GLASS PENDANT
30x30mm sea glass focal, undrilled
6 ft. 20-gauge copper wire

STONE PENDANT
30x30mm stone nugget
6 ft. 20-gauge copper wire

tools
Annealing toolkit, p. 17
Bail-making pliers
Roundnose pliers
Chasing hammer
Steel block
Wire cutters
Chainnose pliers
Finishing toolkit, p. 23 (optional)

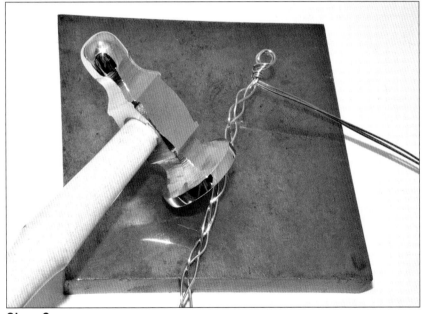

Step 3
Hammer the braided wires on a steel block to flatten them.

This stone is gorgeous, caught in an entangled net...

Step 4

Anneal the braided wires. **Tip: The wire will be brittle due to hammering in Step 3. Annealing the wire will prevent it from breaking as you continue to manipulate it.** If you're working with a fragile stone, place the wires in a pickle solution to remove any oxidation at this point.

Step 5

Place the sea glass or stone nugget over the wire, and begin wrapping the nugget with the braided wires. For a triangle shape, create a "cage" by criss-crossing the braided wire on the back and wrapping once around two corners. When the nugget is caged, wrap the braided wires around the neck of the bail once.

Step 6

Trim the excess braided wires. Use the remaining wires to wrap the top of the nugget. If desired, trim the wires and stop here (as shown in the Stone Pendant). For the Sea Glass Pendant, trim the vertical wires to 2 in.

Step 7

Make a flat spiral with each of the remaining wires (see p. 15). Place the spirals on the front of the piece as desired.

Step 8

Place the piece in a pickle solution to remove any oxidation if you didn't in Step 4. Tumble-polish and add patina as desired (see p. 23).

Castaway
ring

Cast adrift with this spectacular ring! You can showcase a small assortment of sea glass or gemstone chips or coil wire around one main focal piece. We've made this ring with glass, but it would look just as lovely with a gemstone, pearl, or crystal center—or maybe all three!

Step 1

Center and bend the textured wire around the ring mandrel at the desired size.

Step 2

(a) Using heavy-duty flush cutters, carefully trim the textured wire where it meets and file the ends of the band smooth.

(b) Re-align the ends of the band.

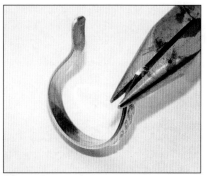

Step 3

(a) One-fourth in. from each end of the band, bend the textured wire 45 degrees with chainnose pliers.

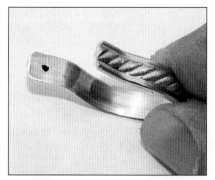

(b) Place a mark ⅛ in. from the end on each side of the band with a permanent marker.

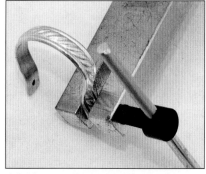

(c) Line up the markings in the screw-action metal punch, and punch holes at each end of the band.

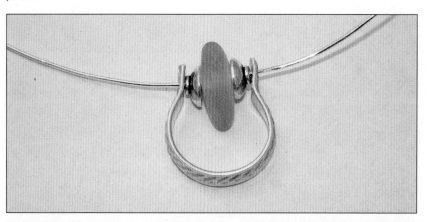

Step 4

String the components on the 20-gauge wire as desired. For the Sea Glass Ring, string a band hole, a bead cap, a sea glass nugget, a bead cap, and the other band hole. For the Round Bead Ring, substitute a 14mm glass rondelle for the nugget. For the Glass Chip Ring, string a band hole, three sea glass chips, and the remaining band hole.

Step 5
Cut the 12-in. coiled wire in half with wire cutters, and trim the ends. On each side of the ring, slide the coiled wire onto the 20-gauge wire.

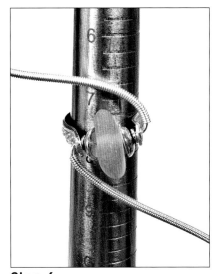

Step 6
(a) Place the entire assembly on the ring mandrel, and wrap each coiled wire end in a windmill motion around the assembly to create a bezel.

(b) When the bezel is the desired size, trim the excess coiled wire, being careful not to cut the 20-gauge wire.

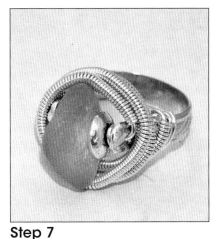

Step 7
At the end of the coiled wire, wrap the 20-gauge wire around the band a few times to anchor it. Trim and tuck the ends. Tumble-polish and add patina as desired (see p. 23).

materials
SEA GLASS RING
20x15mm center-drilled sea glass nugget (see p. 12)

2 6mm silver bead caps

3 in. textured flat silver wire, approx. ¼ in. wide

24 in. 20-gauge silver wire

12 in. 24-gauge coiled silver wire

ROUND BEAD RING
14mm glass rondelle bead

2 10mm silver bead caps

3 in. textured flat silver wire, approx. ¼ in. wide

24 in. 20-gauge silver wire

12 in. 24-gauge coiled silver wire

GLASS CHIP RING
3 8–12mm center-drilled blue and green sea glass chips

3 in. textured flat silver wire, approx. ¼ in. wide

24 in. 20-gauge silver wire

12 in. 24-gauge coiled silver wire

tools
Ring mandrel

Metal file

Heavy-duty flush cutters

Chainnose pliers

Permanent marker

Metal punch

Rubber mallet

Finishing toolkit, p. 23 (optional)

Catch a Wave
cuff and collar

You'll be all set for a day at the beach with these casual pieces. Choose sea glass nuggets offset by dark copper wire or select ceramic beads with aluminum wire for a large-but-lightweight collar. This is the perfect project for practicing your drilling skills!

materials

SEA GLASS AND COPPER CUFF

6-10 25–30mm rounded coin-shaped side-drilled sea glass beads (see p. 12)

5 ft. 12-gauge copper wire

CERAMIC AND ALUMINUM COLLAR

12-14 25–30mm ceramic beads

5 ft. 12-gauge aluminum wire

Note: The holes in your beads or glass must be large enough to accommodate 12-gauge wire: approximately 2mm.

tools

Permanent marker

Tape measure

Nylon-jaw pliers

Wire cutters

Roundnose pliers

Bracelet mandrel or neck form

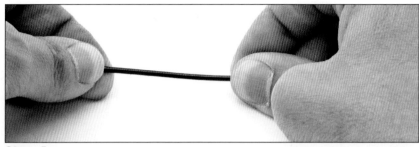

Step 1

Straighten the wire with nylon-jaw pliers.

Step 2

Mark the center of the wire with a permanent marker. Center all sea glass or ceramic beads on the wire. For a 6½-in. average wrist size, the length of beads on the wire should be approximately 6 in. For a 15–16-in. collar, you'll need approximately 13–14 in. of beads.

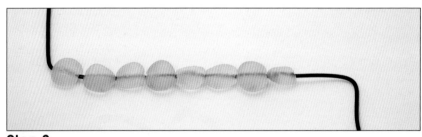

Step 3

Working from left to right, bend the wire 90 degrees up. Approximately ¾ in. away from the last bead on the right, bend the wire 90 degrees down.

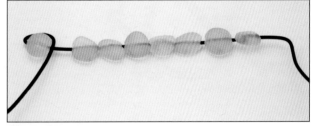

Step 4

(a) Beginning on the left, wrap the wire up and over the top of the first bead, and down between the first and second bead.

(b) Coil the wire end between the first and second bead one full rotation, being sure to keep the coils tightly together. The wire end will now be pointing down.

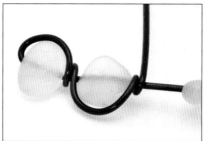

Tip: The most challenging part of this project is getting the wire to stay over the top and bottom of the bead instead of sliding forward to the front of the bead. To avoid this, hold the wire tightly in position at all times while wrapping.

Step 5

(a) Slide the second bead to the left. Hold the first and second bead together, and wrap the wire under the bottom of the second bead.

(b) Coil the wire end one full rotation between the second and third bead. The wire will now be facing up.

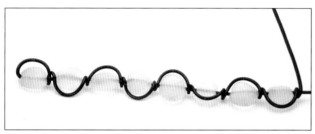

Step 6

Slide the next bead to the left, and continue wrapping until all of the beads are wrapped.

Step 7

Trim the wrapped wire from left to right, as shown. Tip: Trimming at the top or bottom will keep the end of the wire from scratching when you wear the finished piece.

Step 8

Gently compress the end of the wire with nylon-jaw pliers.

Step 9

(a) Begin working from right to left with the other end of the wire. Wrap the wire up and over OR down and under (see Tip below) the first bead.

(b) Coil the wire a full rotation over the top of the existing wire coil. The wire will now be facing up or down, depending on whether you've used an even or an odd number of beads. Tip: When using odd numbers of beads, the first wrapping from right to left will go down. When using even numbers of beads, the first wrap from right to left will go up.

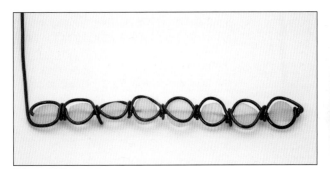

Step 10
Continue wrapping from right to left until all of the beads are wrapped.

Step 11
Trim the remaining wire to 3 in. Create a space by inserting the tip of the roundnose pliers into the space between the wire and the first bead on the left. If the space is too small, enlarge the space by gently moving the tip of the pliers back and forth.

Step 12
Coil the wire two full rotations into the space by gently pulling and turning the wire through the coil with the pliers.

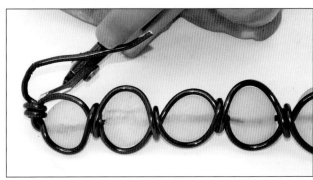

Step 13
Trim the wire (see Step 7).

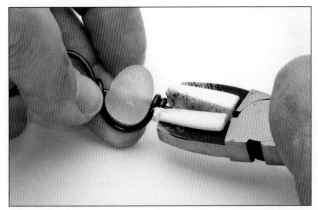

Step 14
Gently compress the wire end with nylon-jaw pliers.

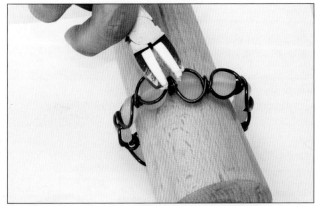

Step 15
Bend the piece around the bracelet mandrel or neck form to the desired shape and size. As you shape the piece, the coils may spread apart. If that happens, gently squeeze the coils together with the nylon-jaw pliers.

Vortex
earrings

Large swirls of silver make these earrings perfect for a special occasion. Use big, creamy pearls for earrings that will go with anything or wrap red nuggets for an unexpected splash of color. We've made this project with both drilled and undrilled pieces, so use whatever size or shape you like!

materials

PEARL EARRINGS

2 12mm white glass pearls

2 6mm clear bicone crystals

22 in. 18-gauge square silver wire

2 2-in. silver headpins

Pair of silver earring wires

GLASS EARRINGS

2 12x5mm red glass nugget, undrilled

2 6mm clear round crystals

22 in. 18-gauge square silver wire

2 2-in. silver headpins

Pair of silver earring wires

tools

Permanent marker

Tape measure

Wire cutters

Chainnose pliers

Chasing hammer

Steel block

Roundnose pliers

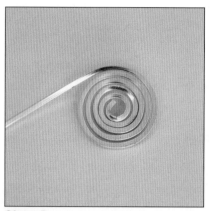

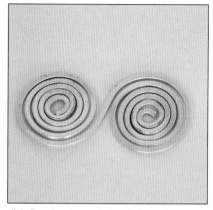

Step 1

(a) Cut an 11-in. piece of 18-gauge square wire. Mark the centerpoint of the wire with a permanent marker. Beginning at one end of the wire, create a flat spiral (see p. 15), stopping when you reach the center mark.

(b) Beginning at the opposite end of the wire, create another flat spiral going in the opposite direction. The two spirals will meet in the middle. **Tip: Make sure the square wire has not twisted. You want a nice, smooth line.**

Step 2

Work-harden and flatten the spiral by hammering on a steel block with the flat face of a chasing hammer.

Step 3

(a) Using chainnose pliers, carefully fold the spiral in half at the centerpoint.

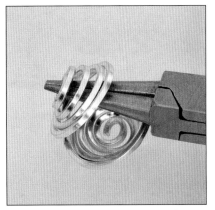

(b) Using the tip of your round-nose pliers, poke the center of the spiral outward on each side.

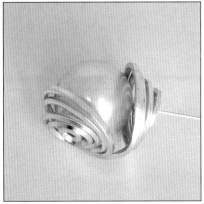

Step 4

Insert the pearl or nugget into the folded spiral. If you are using a pearl or other bead with a hole, string a headpin through the pearl so the headpin exits the top of the folded spiral.

Step 5

Close the spiral. If you are using an undrilled nugget, grasp the top of the bead cage, where the small loop sits on the spiral, and bend it 90 degrees; make a wrapped loop on one end of a headpin, and attach it to the small loop.

Step 6

String a crystal on the headpin and make a wire-wrapped loop.

Step 7

Attach the wrapped loop to the earring wire. Repeat Steps 1–7 to make a second earring.

Flower Cup
ring

Cheerful enameled components brighten up any design
with a burst of color. Choose a monochromatic palette
by matching lime sea glass and forest-green enamel
or embrace contrast with stacked yellow and purple
enamel dotted with a creamy pearl.

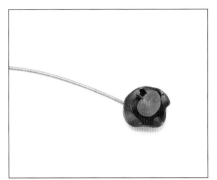

Step 1

Create a 12-in. wire coil with the 24-gauge wire (see p. 16). Ball one end of the 20-gauge wire (see p. 19). String the components and coiled wire onto the balled wire. For the Sea Glass Ring, string the sea glass nugget and the 25mm floral component. For the Pearl Ring, string the 8mm pearl, the 20mm floral component, and the 25mm floral component.

Step 2

On the ring mandrel, at the desired ring size, complete two full wraps with the coiled assembly. Wrap the coiled wire under the final floral component once.

materials

SEA GLASS RING

25mm enameled copper floral component

10mm (approx.) center-drilled sea glass nugget (see p. 12)

2 ft. 20-gauge copper wire

12 ft. 24-gauge copper wire

PEARL RING

25mm enameled copper floral component

20mm enameled copper floral component

8mm white pearl

2 ft. 20-gauge copper wire

12 ft. 24-gauge copper wire

Note: We found these enameled components at C-Koop Beads.

tools

Coiling Wire toolkit, p. 16

Annealing toolkit, p. 17

Wire cutters

Ring mandrel

Roundnose pliers

Chainnose pliers

Finishing toolkit, p. 23 (optional)

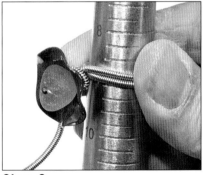

Step 3

Work-harden the ring shank by twisting and pushing downward at the same time. Remove the ring, reverse, and repeat.

Step 4

Continue wrapping the coiled wire under the enameled component, as shown. For the Pearl Ring, wrap the floral component only once, and then wrap the remaining coils around the band next to the component. Tip: If you like, make a small swirl on the ring band with the excess wire.

Step 5

With the remaining 20-gauge wire, wrap the band. Trim and tuck any excess wire. Tumble-polish and add patina as desired (see p. 23).

Under the Sea
pendant

A hint of color peeks through copper mesh in this playful pendant. The green of a sea glass nugget is a sharp contrast to patinated copper, but you could also choose a glass drop with hints of copper foil for a warm, harmonious look.

Step 1
Cut two 1-in. diameter copper disks with the disk cutter.

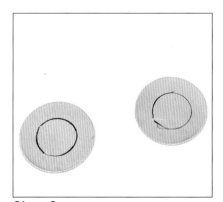

Step 2
(a) Draw a ½-in. diameter circle in the center of each disk with the permanent marker.

(b) Punch a ½-in. diameter hole with the disk cutter to create a washer.

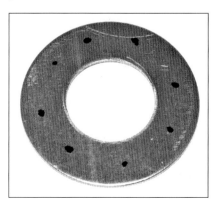

Step 3
With the permanent marker, make eight evenly spaced marks around one disk. These will become holes, so center them in the washer. Tip: Begin by marking the top of the disk, and then mark the bottom. Then mark the right and left sides. Add the final marks between the top/right/bottom/left marks for nice, even spacing.

materials
SEA GLASS PENDANT
4–6mm sea glass nugget, undrilled

2 1½x1½-in. pieces of 24-gauge copper sheet

2 1½x1½-in. pieces of light-gauge copper mesh

8mm copper jump ring

7 brass micro screws (1.3x10mm long), including washers and nuts

FOILED GLASS PENDANT
4–6mm foiled glass drop

2 1½x1½-in. pieces of 24-gauge copper sheet

2 1½x1½-in. pieces of light-gauge copper mesh

8mm copper jump ring

7 brass micro screws (1.3x10mm long), including washers and nuts

Note: The copper wire mesh used in this project is 3000 series WireKnitZ.

tools
Disk cutter

Household hammer

Permanent marker

Awl

Scissors

1.5mm metal hole punch

Wire cutters

Metal file

Finishing toolkit, p. 23 (optional)

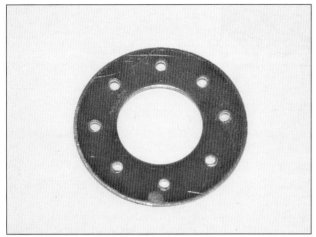

Step 4

(a) Punch each marked hole with the hole punch.

(b) Stack the two disks, and using the holes on the top disk as a guide, punch holes in the bottom disk. To keep the disks aligned while punching holes, connect the two disks with the jump ring at the first hole.

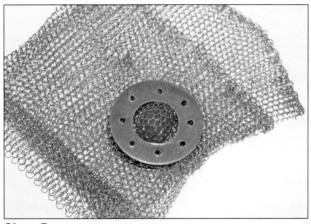

Step 5

Remove the jump ring. Layer the top disk, a piece of copper wire mesh, the sea glass nugget or glass drop, the other piece of mesh, and the bottom disk. Punch through the mesh, and re-align the holes with the awl. Use rivets to keep the holes aligned and temporarily hold the layered pieces in place.

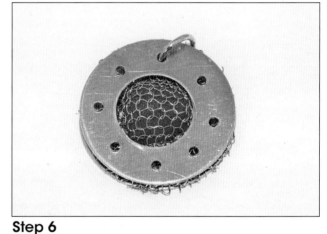

Step 6

Trim the excess mesh with scissors, and insert the jump ring in the top hole. Insert the micro screws in the remaining holes. Place the washer and the nut on the opposite side, and tighten. Trim the excess screw with wire cutters and file, if required. Tumble-polish and add patina as desired (see p. 23).

Water Lily Bouquet
pendant

Sometimes one flower isn't enough; that's where this pendant comes in! Keep it simple with three multicolored blooms, as in the enameled flower bouquet, or add swirls of wire and lots of colorful chips, as in the sea glass pendant. Use these materials lists as a guideline, and select the number of blooms that best fits your mood.

SEA GLASS PENDANT

30x20mm yellow enameled cone

5 10–12mm center-drilled sea glass chips (see p. 12)

5 6–8mm center-drilled sea glass chips

20 in. 24-gauge copper coiled wire

36 in. 20-gauge copper wire

3 6mm copper jump rings

ENAMELED FLOWER PENDANT

40x20mm brown enameled cone

3 8mm enameled flower components

3 4mm enameled flower components

18 in. 24-gauge copper coiled wire

30 in. 20-gauge copper wire

3 6mm copper jump rings

Note: The enameled components used in this project are by C-Koop Beads.

tools

Coiling Wire toolkit, p. 16

Wire cutters

Roundnose pliers

Chainnose pliers

Step 1

For the Sea Glass Pendant, cut five 1–1½ in. wire coils and six 6-in. pieces of 20-gauge wire. For the Enameled Flower Pendant, cut three wire coils and four 6-in. pieces of wire.

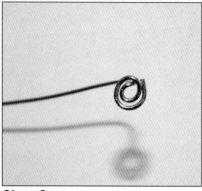

Step 2

Make a small, centered, flat spiral on the end of a piece of 20-gauge wire (see p. 15). Repeat four times for the Sea Glass Pendant, two times for the Enameled Flower Pendant.

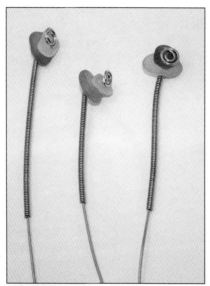

Step 3

For the Sea Glass Pendant: On a 6-in. piece of 20-gauge wire. string a 6–8mm sea glass, a 10–12mm sea glass, and a coiled wire; repeat four times. For the Enameled Flower Pendant: On a 6-in. piece of 20-gauge wire, string a 4mm flower component, an 8mm flower component, and a wire coil; repeat twice.

Step 4

Place the coiled wire assemblies into the cone as desired, with the wire ends protruding from the bottom. Fold the wire ends up over the front of the cone, and trim to ½ in.

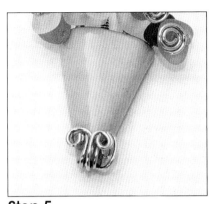

Step 5
Create a small, flat spiral on each wire end.

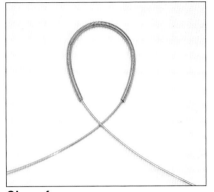

Step 6
Center 3 in. of coiled wire on a 6-in. piece of 20-gauge wire, and loop as shown. Tip: If your cone has holes on each side, you will only need 3 in. of 20-gauge wire. After stringing the coiled wire, string both holes on the cone from the outside in. Twist the wire ends together inside the cone to secure. Using this method, you can skip Step 7.

*Ah, Monet.
If only you had
included sea glass...*

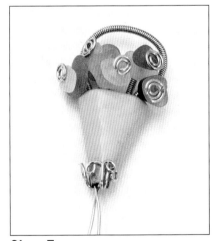

Step 7
(a) Pull the ends of the 20-gauge wire through the bottom of the cone.

(b) Repeat Step 5.

Step 8
Attach three jump rings to the coiled wire handle. String a chain through the jump rings to create a necklace with the pendant.

Intermediate
projects

Bubble Wrap
pendant

Sometimes less is more—and sometimes more is better! Wrap an undrilled stone with crystal and pearls for a polished presentation. Add a banner of beads to the right or to the left of your stone, and create spirals on the top—as many or as few as you like—to complete the look.

Step 1

Cut the 21-gauge wire into three 14-in. pieces. Stack the wires (these are called the wrapping wires). Mark the center of the stacked wires with a permanent marker. Place painters tape on each side of the mark.

Step 2

(a) Cut four 4-in. pieces of 18-gauge wire (these are called the binding wires). Hook one binding wire around the wrapping wires as shown.

(b) Wrap the binding wire, compressing after each wrap with the nylon-jaw pliers. Trim excess binding wire from the inside. Tip: The number of wraps will depend on the focal size; for best results, we recommend using an odd number of wraps.

materials

GLASS PENDANT

20x40mm (approx.) undrilled sea glass focal

3 6mm orange bicone crystals

4 3–4mm silver barrel-shaped rice pearls

6 2–3mm silver spacers

16 in. 18-gauge half-round silver wire

42 in. 21-gauge half-hard square silver wire

STONE PENDANT

40mm (approx.) stone cabochon

3 4mm red bicone crystals

3 3–4mmmm copper barrels

7 2–3mm copper spacers

16 in. 18-gauge half-round copper wire

42 in. 21-gauge half-hard square copper wire

Note: All of the beads must fit on 21-gauge square wire.

tools

Permanent marker

Tape measure

Painters tape

Nylon-jaw pliers

Wire cutters

Chainnose pliers

Roundnose pliers

Step 3

(a) Place the focal stone or glass flat on the wires, and bend the wrapping wires up.

(b) Determine the location of the binding wire on each side of the focal, and mark the wrapping wires with a permanent marker. Above the mark, place painters tape on both sides of the wrapping wires.

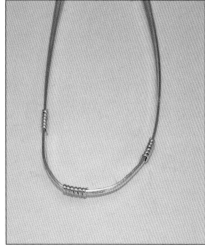

Step 4

Repeat Step 2 on both sides. Remove the painters tape. Use the same number of wraps for each binding wire.

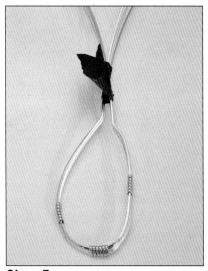

Step 5

Bend the wrapping wires around the top of the focal so both sets of wrapping wires meet in the middle. Bend the wrapping wires with the chainnose pliers, and tape the two sections of wrapping wires together.

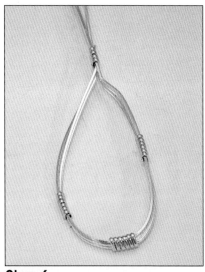

Step 6

Repeat Step 2 at the top of the piece, and remove the painters tape.

Step 7

Place the focal into the wrapping wires. Bring the first wire in the center of each quadrant (the four spaces between each wrap) forward with the tip of the roundnose pliers. Repeat on the back side.

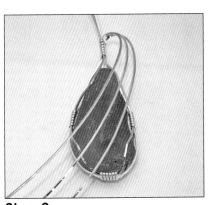

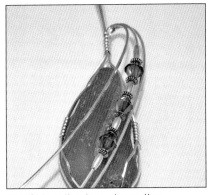

Step 8

(a) Choose three wrapping wires from the left or right, and pull down and across the front of the focal to create a banner.

(b) String the beads on the center wrapping wire in the desired pattern until the last bead reaches the lower edge of the glass. Tip: Start and end with the same bead.

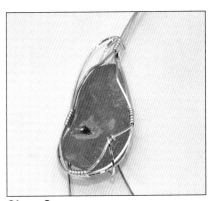

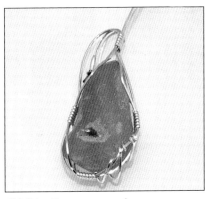

Step 9

(a) Bend the center wrapping wire to the back. Attach the center wrapping wire to the back by hooking it around the back quadrant wrapping wire, as shown.

(b) Trim the excess wire.

(c) Repeat with the remaining two wrapping wires.

Step 10

(a) Choose one of the remaining wrapping wires, and make a wire-wrapped loop for the bail (see p. 14).

(b) Trim the ends of the remaining wires to approximately 1½ in., and create 2–4 flat spirals (see p. 15). Place the spirals against the focal as desired.

Day at the Beach
charm bracelet

With this project, you can choose whatever stones, crystals, pearls, sea glass nuggets, or other found objects you like to complete a sweet charm bracelet. Follow our lead or create your very own treasure trove for your wrist!

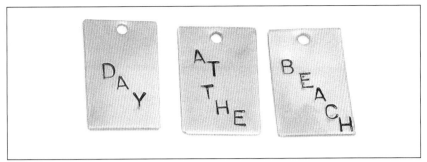

Step 1

Stamp a beach-themed sentiment on the three metal blanks (see p. 22). Punch a hole at the top of each piece.

(see p. 22)

materials

CHARM BRACELET

6 top-drilled (front-to-back) sea glass nuggets (see p. 12)

3 ½ x1-in.18-gauge copper blanks

13 10mm cornflake beads

13 6mm round beads

13 2mm round beads

4 miscellaneous beach-themed charms

3 7-in. charm chains in different metals and links sizes/shapes

11 8mm copper jump rings

15 4mm copper jump rings

13 2-in. headpins

Two-part S-hook clasp

tools

Stamping Metal toolkit, p. 22

Wire cutters

Roundnose pliers and a second pair of pliers

1.5mm metal hole punch

(see p. 12)

Step 2

Using 8mm jump rings, attach the three stamped pieces to one of the three chains (this is the working chain), spacing them evenly.

Step 3

Use 4mm jump rings to attach beach-themed charms to the working chain.

Step 4

Use 8mm jump rings to attach top-drilled sea glass nuggets to the working chain.

Step 5

String a 2mm round bead, a cornflake bead, and a 6mm round bead on a headpin. Make a wire-wrapped loop (see p. 14). Repeat to make a total of 13 dangles.

Wear memories of summer days at the beach on your wrist, all year 'round.

Step 6

Use 4mm jump rings to attach the dangles to the working chain as desired. **Tip: Try placing the dangles randomly for an organic feel.**

Step 7

Use an 8mm jump ring to attach all three chains at one end. Repeat on the other end. Attach half of an S-hook closure to an 8mm jump ring at each end of the bracelet.

Rockin' Riveted
ring

Show off this rockin' ring made with a sturdy textured band. A burst of color peeks through the copper: either an unusual piece of red sea glass, or a sparkly, modern crystal rondelle. You could also use multiple pieces of glass, a combination of spacers, or any center-drilled stone for this simple-but-chic construction.

materials

GLASS RING

10–12mm (approx.) center-drilled sea glass nugget (see p. 12)

4 in. 20-gauge ¼-in. copper sheet

½-in. 1.3mm copper nailhead rivet

4mm copper daisy spacer bead

CRYSTAL RING

10–12mm clear crystal rondelle

4 in. 20-gauge ¼-in. copper sheet

½-in. 1.3mm copper nailhead rivet

tools

Annealing toolkit, p. 17

Texture hammer

Steel block

Metal shears

Metal file

Ring mandrel

1.5mm metal hole punch

Permanent marker

Brass brush

Wire cutters

Chasing hammer

Finishing toolkit, p. 23 (optional)

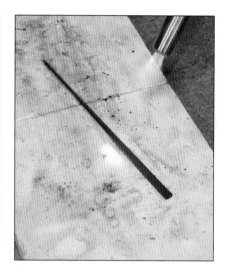

Step 1
Anneal the metal sheet and remove any firescale (see p. 17).

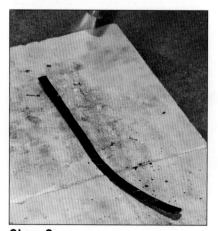

Step 2
Texture the metal sheet with a texture hammer (see p. 21). File the edges, if required. **Tip: If you prefer, you can begin with textured sheet metal and skip this step.**

Step 3
(a) Re-anneal the metal sheet.

(b) Straighten the metal sheet by hammering with a rawhide mallet.

Step 4

Trim two metal corners on one end of the band with the metal shears to create slightly rounded edges, and file the rounded edges with the metal file.

Step 5

At the desired ring size, shape the band on the mandrel as shown. The band will start to overlap itself on the mandrel, so leave about a ¼-in. gap between the curved end of the wrapped band and the remaining length of the band.

Step 6

Punch a hole ⅛ in. from the end of the formed band (the end with the rounded corners) with the metal hole punch.

Step 7

(a) Place a rivet through the hole.

(b) Place a sea glass or crystal focal on the rivet, place the assembly back on the mandrel, and bend the remaining band length over the top of the focal.

(c) Use a permanent marker to mark a second hole centered over the focal.

Step 8
(a) Remove the assembly from the mandrel, and remove the focal and rivet.

(b) Punch the second hole at the marked spot.

Step 9
About ⅛ in. beyond the second hole, trim the band, and round both remaining corners as in Step 4.

Step 10
Place the band in the pickle to remove any firescale. Remove the band from the pickle, and polish with a brass brush.

Step 11
(a) Put the rivet through the bottom hole of the band, and string through the focal and the top hole of the band.

(b) Place the assembly on the ring mandrel.

Step 12
(a) Add a spacer bead, if desired. Trim the rivet to ¹⁄₁₆ in. above the assembly (approximately the thickness of a credit card).

(b) Carefully spread the other end of the rivet with a chasing hammer. Tumble-polish and add patina as desired (see p. 23).

Swirling Seas
bangle

Swirling copper wire atop a lovely beach gem makes a magnificent bangle—and this piece is elegant even without an accent bead. We made both pieces in copper to embrace and celebrate our favorite metal.

SEA GLASS BANGLE

25mm (approx.) center-drilled
   sea glass nugget (see p. 12)

42 in. 14-gauge wire

5mm grommet

Jewelers glue (optional)

PLAIN COPPER BANGLE

42 in. 14-gauge wire

tools

Annealing toolkit, p. 17

Setting a Grommet toolkit,
   p. 13 (Sea Glass Bangle only)

Oval bracelet mandrel

Rubber mallet

Heavy duty wire cutters

Nylon-jaw pliers

Brass brush

Finishing toolkit, p. 23 (optional)

Step 1

If you are using a sea glass nugget, drill a 5mm hole in the nugget and insert a grommet (see p. 13). If the grommet is too big, put a drop of jewelers glue on the lip of the grommet before setting it in the glass.

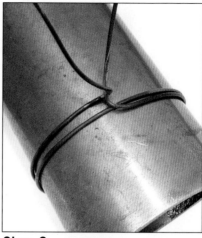

Step 2

Anneal the 14-gauge wire. Center the wire on the front of the mandrel at the desired bangle size. Wrap the wire around the mandrel, and bring both wire ends back to the front, making sure to keep the wires around the mandrel parallel. Twist the wires together in the front.

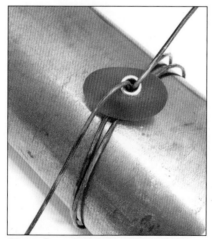

Step 3

Hammer the wire with a rubber mallet to work-harden the bangle. If using a nugget, slide the nugget onto the wires at this point. Spread the wires apart.

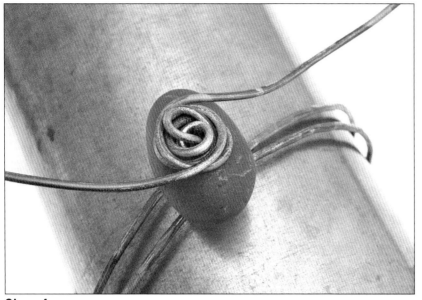

Embrace design possibilities when projects don't go exactly as planned. You never know what you may create!

Step 4

Create a rosette shape by wrapping the wire ends in a windmill fashion. Don't make your wraps extremely tight, but don't allow much space between the wraps, either.

Step 6

Place the bangle in a pickle solution to remove any firescale. Polish the piece with a brass brush. Tumble-polish and add patina as desired (see p. 23).

Step 5

Anchor the wires by wrapping one wire end around the bangle on each side of the center rosette. Trim the excess wire. Use nylon-jaw pliers to compress the coils together.

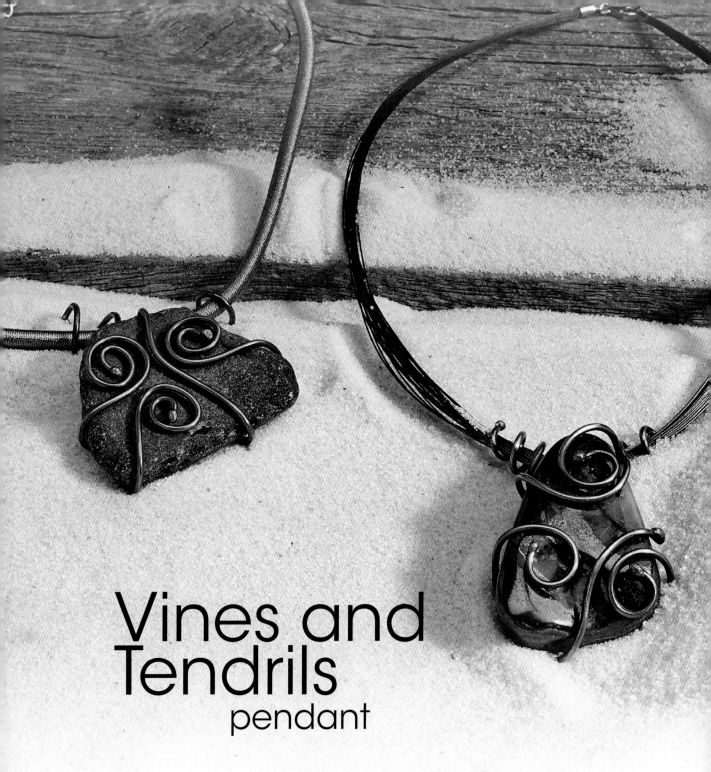

Vines and Tendrils
pendant

Ensnare a triangular stone or a freeform chunk of glass in this clever capture. Create swirls as desired on the front and use your torch to melt wire and ensure a secure fit on the back.

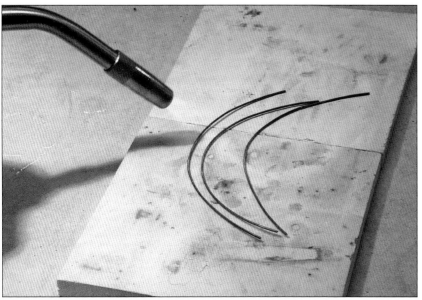

Step 1

Cut the 16-gauge wire into three 8-in. pieces. Anneal and quench (see p. 17).

(see p. 17)

materials

GLASS PENDANT

30x45mm (approx.) undrilled sea glass nugget

24 in. 16-gauge copper wire

copper brazing rod

STONE PENDANT

30x40mm (approx.) undrilled stone nugget

24 in. 16-gauge copper wire

copper brazing rod

tools

Annealing toolkit, p. 17

Tape measure

Permanent marker

Wire cutters

Pen

Finishing toolkit, p. 23 (optional)

Annealing toolkit, p. 17 ... Finishing toolkit, p. 23 (optional)

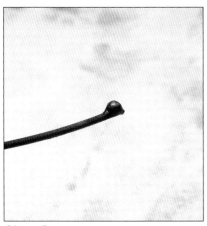

Step 2

Ball up each end on all three wires (see p. 19).

(see p. 19)

Step 3

Bend each wire into a "U" shape, and lay together on the solder board so they are touching in the middle.

This design was inspired by jewelry designer Margo Farrin-O'Connor.

Step 4
Braze three pieces of wire so they are connected (see p. 20). Quench.

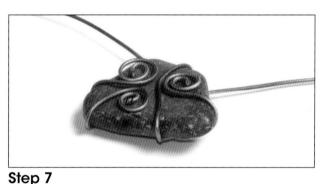

Step 5
Place the sea glass or stone focal on the brazed wires in the desired orientation.

Step 6
Wrap one bottom-side wire across the front of the focal to anchor the focal in place. **Tip: Depending on the width and size of your focal, the wire may not wrap all the way around it. That's OK—just be sure to anchor the stone well in the remaining steps.**

Step 7
Bring three more wires (from the remaining bottom side and middle positions) to the front. Make flat spirals (see p. 15), positioned as desired across the front of the focal. For the triangle-shaped stone, we placed one spiral at the top and two at the bottom corners. For the trapezoid-shaped sea glass, we placed two spirals at the top and one near the bottom center.

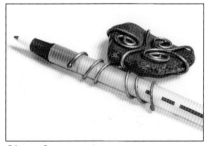

Step 8
Wrap the two remaining wires (from the top positions) around a pen or other dowel three or four times, leaving about 5mm between each wrap, to create a bail.

Step 9
Remove the pen, and adjust the wires. Pickle the piece to remove any firescale. Tumble-polish and add patina as desired (see p. 23).

Eye of the Storm
cuff

If you're looking for a truly distinctive piece, this cuff offers both heft and wild beauty. We love the look of turquoise and sea glass against copper, but you could also showcase silver or bronze wire. Either way, this piece, created in a maelstrom of wirewrapping, is sure to draw attention.

materials

TURQUOISE CUFF

40x30mm side-drilled turquoise focal

15 ft. 14-gauge copper wire

4 ft. 16-gauge copper wire

SEA GLASS CUFF

40x30mm double-drilled sea glass focal (see p. 12)

15 ft. 14-gauge copper wire

4 in. 16-gauge copper wire

tools

Annealing toolkit, p. 17

Measuring tape

Permanent marker

Rubber mallet

Heavy-duty flush cutters

Oval bracelet mandrel

Chasing hammer

Roundnose pliers

Finishing toolkit, p. 23 (optional)

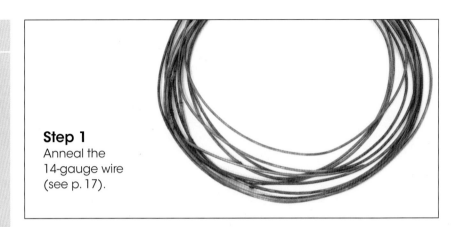

Step 1
Anneal the 14-gauge wire (see p. 17).

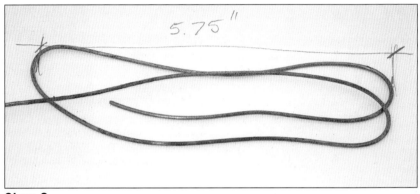

Step 2
Measure your wrist, and create a template that is the same length. Create the base of the cuff by wrapping one end of the 14-gauge wire back and forth on the template three times.

Step 3
Wrap the remaining wire loosely around the base in a random pattern. Tuck the end of the wire to the inside. **Tip: When you are wrapping, go all the way to each end.**

Step 4
Hammer the wrapped wire flat with a rubber mallet.

Step 5

(a) If the piece has "grown", use the roundnose pliers to bend the end pieces toward the center until you are back to the original size.

(b) Hammer the wrapped wire from the top and bottom with the rubber mallet to make the width of the bracelet even.

(c) Verify that the piece is back to the original size. Tip: Re-anneal, if necessary, so you are able to continue shaping the wire.

Step 6

(a) Bend the piece around the mandrel.

(b) Use a rubber mallet to shape and work-harden the piece, and to form a cuff.

(c) Hammer the wrapped wire from the top and bottom with the rubber mallet to even out the width of the bracelet.

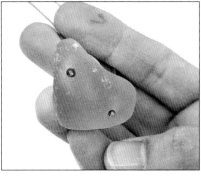

Step 7

Place the cuff in a pickle solution to remove any firescale. Remove from the pickle solution, rinse, and polish with a brass brush.

Step 8

For a side-drilled focal, center it on a 4-ft. piece of 16-gauge wire. For a double-drilled focal, cut the 16-gauge wire into two 24-in. pieces. Ball one end of each wire (see p. 19). Insert the other wire ends into the two holes of the turquoise or sea glass focal, from front to back.

Step 9
(a) Attach the focal by sliding each wire end through the center of the cuff.

(b) Cross the wires on the inside of the cuff.

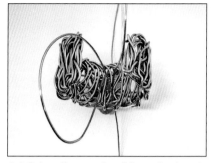

(c) Bring the ends of the wire back through the cuff to the front.

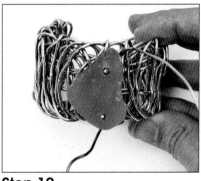

Step 10
(a) Wrap the wire ends around the focal in a windmill fashion to create a bezel.

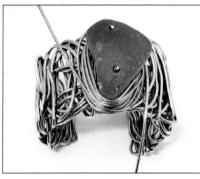

(b) Stop when you are happy with the size of the bezel.

Step 11
Tuck the ends of the wire back through the cuff to the inside. Trim the wires to ½ in. Work the ends of the wires into the cuff with round-nose pliers. Make sure the ends of the wires are not poking out from either side of the cuff.

Step 12
Tumble-polish and add patina as desired (see p. 23).

Creating "sheet" from wire was our accidental discovery. The malformed wire was hammered flat out of exasperation, which led to an "aha" moment.

Cocktails on the Beach
ring

Perfect for drinks on the beach at dusk, this coiled ring is accented with plenty of eye-catching sparkle. Choose silver and rich, blue sea glass for a classic palette or evoke the warm colors of the sunset with multiple crystal shades and a copper setting.

materials

SEA GLASS AND SILVER RING

20mm (approx.) round center-drilled sea glass focal (see p. 12)

30 in. 20-gauge silver wire

30 in. 22-gauge silver wire

30 in. 26-gauge silver wire

24 3mm bicone crystals

25 2mm silver spacer beads

6mm silver daisy spacer bead

CRYSTAL AND COPPER RING

12mm amber crystal rondelle focal

30 in. 20-gauge copper wire

30 in. 22-gauge copper wire

30 in. 26-gauge copper wire

24 3mm red bicone crystals

25 2mm copper spacer beads

4mm copper daisy spacer bead

Note: All crystals and spacers must be able to fit on the 20-gauge wire.

tools

Annealing toolkit, p. 17

Wire cutter

Tape measure

Permanent marker

Ring mandrel

Rubber mallet

Chainnose pliers

Finishing toolkit, p. 23 (optional)

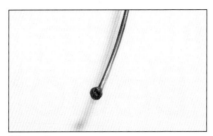

Step 1
Ball up one end of the 20-gauge wire (see p. 19).

Step 2
Slide a daisy spacer bead and the sea glass or crystal focal onto the 20-gauge balled wire (the balled end will act as a stopper). Bend the wire flat against the focal with chainnose pliers as shown.

Step 3
Place the wire on the mandrel, with the focal at the top, at one size larger than the desired finished size.

Step 4
(a) Wrap the 20-gauge wire around the ring mandrel, and anchor the wire under the focal by making one wrap underneath it.

(b) Wrap around the mandrel in the opposite direction, and anchor the wire on the opposite side of the focal as in Step 4a. As you wrap, keep the wires parallel and close together.

(c) Wrap the wire around the mandrel again in the first direction, and anchor it on the first side one more time. Repeat Step 4b. Strike the shank with a rubber mallet to work-harden.

Step 5
Wrap the wire under the focal several times.

Step 6
Anchor the end of the 20-gauge wire by wrapping it around the shank once or twice near the focal. Make these few wraps neat and close together. Trim the excess wire.

Step 7
(a) Anchor one end of the 22-gauge wire by wrapping it around the ring shank a few times near the focal, next to the 20-gauge wire wraps.

(b) Alternating between crystals and spacers, string all of the beads on the 22-gauge wire. Place the ring on the mandrel and wrap the wire with crystals and spacer beads to form a bezel. Add or remove crystals and spacers as necessary to fit. Our bezels wrap around the focal multiple times. Anchor the wire end to the shank on the opposite side, and trim the excess wire.

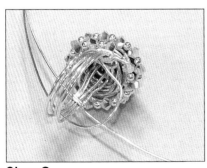

Step 8
Strike the shank with a rubber mallet. Remove it from the mandrel.

Step 9
(a) Beginning at one side of the ring shank, anchor and wrap the 26-gauge wire.

(b) Wrap the wire continuously around the shank, squeezing with chainnose pliers after each wrap. When wrapping is complete, anchor the 26-gauge wire at the opposite end.

Step 10
Place the ring on the ring mandrel, and hammer with a rubber mallet. Tumble-polish and add patina as desired (see p. 23).

Sand Dune
cuff

Any center-drilled bead or nugget will feel right at home in this cool copper cuff. Choose small heishi turquoise beads, or select larger sea glass nuggets. With this adaptable design, it's not size that counts—but quantity!

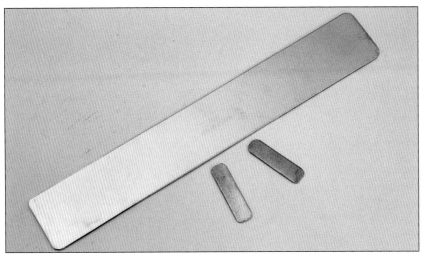

Step 1

Round the corners of all three blanks with metal shears, and file the corners until they're smooth. Make the rounded corners as even and uniform as possible.

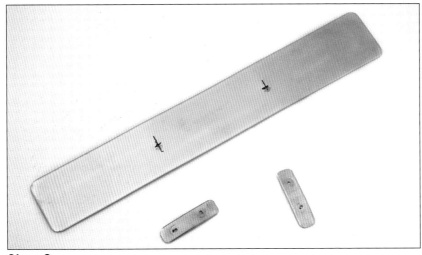

Step 2

With a permanent marker, mark the small (¼x1-in.) metal blanks ¼ in. from each end, centered from top to bottom. Mark the large (1x6-in.) metal blank at 2 in. and 4 in., centered from top to bottom. (This divides the cuff into thirds.) Punch holes in the blanks where marked.

materials

SEA GLASS CUFF

8-12 10–15mm center-drilled sea glass nuggets (see p. 12)

1x6-in. 20-gauge copper blank

2 ¼x1-in. 20-gauge copper blanks

12 in. 18-gauge copper wire

9-13 8mm flat copper disks

2 1.3mm nailhead rivets

TURQUOISE CUFF

12-15 6mm center-drilled turquoise heishi beads

1x6-in. 20-gauge copper blank

2 ¼x1-in. 20-gauge copper blanks

12 in. 18-gauge copper wire

13-16 8mm wavy copper disks

2 1.3mm nailhead rivets

tools

Annealing toolkit, p. 17

Tape measure

Permanent marker

Metal shears

Metal file

1.5mm metal hole punch

Pair of flatnose pliers

Bracelet mandrel

Rubber mallet

Chasing hammer

Finishing toolkit, p. 23 (optional)

Step 3

Using two pairs of flatnose pliers, bend the small metal blanks to form right angles. For the Turquoise Cuff, we bent the blank 1/3 of the way from one end. For the Sea Glass Cuff, we bent the blank in half.

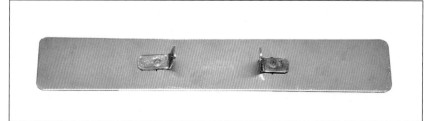

Step 4

Place a hole of a small blank over a hole in the large blank, and connect with a nailhead rivet (see p. 22). Repeat with the second small blank and remaining hole. **Tip: You can rivet through either hole on the small blank. Choose a hole based on the size and number of nuggets or beads.**

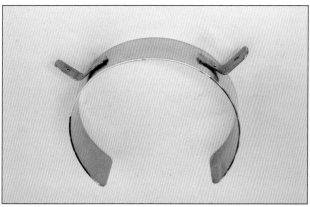

Step 5

Bend the blank around the bracelet mandrel at the desired size to create a cuff. Hammer with a rubber mallet to work-harden.

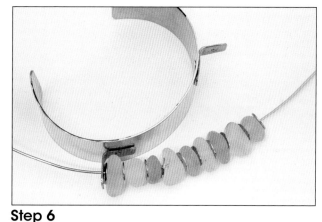

Step 6

Ball one end of the 18-gauge wire (see p. 19). String the wire through the hole of the first small blank. String a disk and a sea glass nugget or turquoise heishi bead on the wire. Continue alternating disks and nuggets or beads until the entire space between the small blanks is filled.

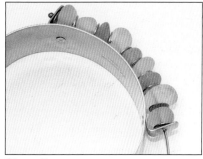

Step 7

String the wire through the hole of the second small blank. Trim the wire to ½ in.

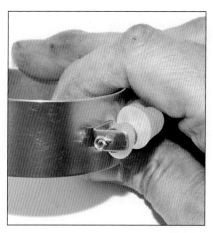

Step 8

Create a small flat spiral to take up the slack in the wire (see p. 15). Fold the spiral tight against the small blank. Tumble-polish and add patina as desired (see p. 23).

Clamshell
bracelet and earrings

Imitate a natural shape in metal with this cool charm-style bracelet. Create domes with silver or copper and accent each metal dome with a burst of color in the form of sea glass or rondelle beads. Accessorize with a pair of earrings to match.

materials

SILVER-AND-BLUE BRACELET

4x3 in. 26-gauge silver sheet

10–12 12mm center-drilled blue sea glass nuggets (see p. 12)

10–12 4mm white pearls

10–12 4mm silver round beads

10–12 4mm silver daisy spacers

7 in. silver charm chain (or size desired)

Silver toggle clasp

20–24 2-in. silver ball-end headpins

2 4mm silver jump rings

COPPER-AND-GREEN BRACELET

4x3 in. 26-gauge copper sheet

10–12 10mm green rondelles

10–12 4mm round beads

10–12 4mm daisy spacers

6 12mm swirl beads

7 in. figure-8 chain (or size desired)

Copper toggle clasp

20–24 2-in. copper ball-end headpins

2 4mm copper jump rings

SILVER-AND-BLUE EARRINGS

1x2 in. 26-gauge silver sheet

2 12mm center-drilled blue sea glass nuggets

2 2-in. silver ball-end headpins

2 4mm silver daisy spacers

2 4mm silver round beads

Pair of silver earring wires

COPPER-AND-GREEN EARRINGS

1x2 in. 26-gauge copper sheet

10–12 10mm green rondelles

2 2-in. copper ball-end headpins

2 links of figure-8 copper chain

2 4mm copper daisy spacers

Pair of copper earring wires

Note: You can create your own ball-end headpins instead of buying them. See p. 19, and begin with a 3-in. length of wire.

tools

⅝-in. disk cutter

Household hammer

Bench block

1.5mm metal hole punch

Tape measure

Dapping set

Permanent marker

Wire cutters

Roundnose pliers

BRACELET
Step 1

Punch 10–12 circles with the ⅝-in. disk cutter, and hammer flat on your bench block. **Tip: If you don't have a disk cutter, you can buy pre-cut disks instead.**

Step 2

Mark the center of each disk with a permanent marker. Punch a hole at each mark with a metal hole punch.

Step 3

Create a bead cap by dapping each disk in the shallowest bowl of a dapping block.

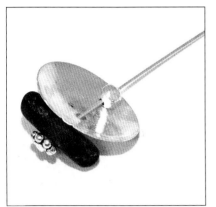

Step 4

(a) On a headpin, string beads and the bead cap you created in Step 3 as desired. For the Silver-and-Blue Bracelet, string a daisy spacer, a sea glass nugget, a bead cap (with the dome facing the nugget), and a round spacer bead. For the Copper-and-Green Bracelet, string a bead cap (with the dome facing the ball end of the headpin), a rondelle, and a daisy spacer.

(b) Make the first half of a wire-wrapped loop above the strung beads (see p. 14).

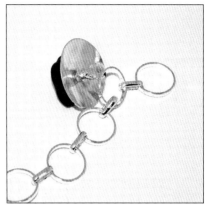

(c) Before finishing the wraps, attach the dangle to the second link in the charm chain. Finish the wraps and trim the excess wire.

Step 5

Repeat Step 4: For the Silver-and-Blue Bracelet, string a pearl and daisy spacer on the headpin. For the Copper-and-Green Bracelet, string a daisy spacer, a spiral bead, and a daisy spacer, or string a daisy spacer and a round bead. Make a wire-wrapped loop. Before finishing the wraps, attach the dangle to a link in the charm chain.

Step 6

Repeat Steps 4 and 5 with the remaining components. Attach half of the toggle clasp to each end of the chain with a jump ring.

EARRINGS
Step 1

Create matching earrings by following Steps 4a and b. Attach an earring wire to each dangle. For the Copper-and-Green Earrings, attached the wrapped loop to a link of figure-8 chain, and attach the earring wire to the other end of the chain link.

Mermaid Tears
collar

This bounty of color and sparkle is a truly freeform way to incorporate various treasures. Choose a color palette of warm burgundy-and-green crystals, and add a hint of wire mesh for a sumptuous feel, or wrap green and blue with silver for a light, bright look.

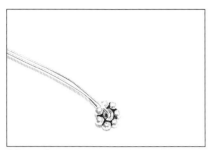

Step 1
Cut 3–4 in. of 26-gauge wire. Center a daisy spacer for the Sea Glass Collar or a loop of crystals in various sizes for the Crystal Collar on the wire. Fold the wire in half.

Step 2
String the sea glass or crystal focal over both wire ends. Wire the focal to the center of the neck collar by wrapping both wire ends around the collar two or three times. Trim the excess wire.

Step 3
For the Sea Glass Collar: With the two remaining wires, repeat Steps 1 and 2 with two sea glass nuggets.

Depending on the beads you choose and their placement, your design may look very different from ours.

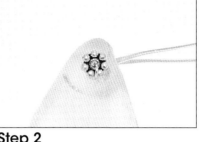

Step 4
For the Sea Glass Collar: Create a cascading bouquet of color by attaching accent beads around the focal in a random fashion with 26-gauge wire. Tip: As you embellish the piece, you can wrap bunches of beads, or wrap a line of beads on the collar with a single piece of wire, or simply wrap one bead at a time. Trim or add wire as needed.

materials

SEA GLASS COLLAR
30x15mm top-drilled (front-to-back) white sea glass focal (see p. 12)

4–6 8–14mm center-drilled blue, green, and white sea glass nuggets

4–6 4mm silver daisy spacers

5–6 8mm blue and green crystal helix beads

1–2 6mm blue bicone crystals

1–3 6mm white crystal pearls

2–3 4mm blue bicone crystals

2–4 2mm gray round beads

Neck collar

3 10-in. pieces 26-gauge coiled silver wire (see p. 16)

4–6 ft. 26-gauge silver wire

4 ft. 20-gauge silver wire

CRYSTAL COLLAR
20mm green briolette crystal focal

8–10 8–14mm top-drilled green, red, and orange bicone crystals

3–4 8mm red rondelle crystals

5–7 6mm gray bicone crystals

3–5 4mm gray bicone crystals

2–4 3mm bicone crystals

16 in. red wire mesh

Neck collar

2 10-in. pieces 26-gauge coiled silver wire

4–6 ft. 26-gauge silver wire

3 ft. 20-gauge silver wire

Note: The wire mesh used in this project is 1000 series WireKnitZ.

tools
Tape measure

Permanent marker

Wire cutter

Awl

Chainnose pliers

Roundnose pliers

Step 5

Cut 2 ft. of 20-gauge wire. Attach the wire to the neck collar above the center assembly by wrapping three times. Trim the excess wire on the short end.

Step 6

Slide the first coil onto the 20-gauge wire. Wrap the entire coil around the neck collar, as shown. **Tip: Skip Step 5 and 6, if desired, anchoring the 20-gauge wire at the top of the neck collar.**

Step 7

Repeat Steps 1 and 2 with more large beads or bead clusters. Position the wrapping wires between the coils to anchor. Trim the excess 26-gauge wire. If wire pokes out, use an awl to push the wire between the coils. Knot wire mesh along the collar at this point, if desired.

Step 8

(a) Slide the second coil on the remaining 20-gauge wire. Loosely coil around both the coiled wire and the focal on the neck collar.

(b) On the back side, anchor and trim the excess 20-gauge wire.

Step 9

Attach another 26-gauge wire on the opposite side of the collar. String beads or attach clusters on the wire, and wrap as desired. Trim the excess wire.

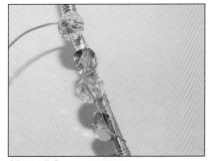

Step 10

With the remaining 20-gauge wire, wrap three coils around the top of the neck collar above the last bead or cluster attached in Step 9. Trim the excess wire.

Step 11

(a) Slide the last coiled wire onto the 20-gauge wire. Wrap loosely to create a vine effect. Wrap the end of the 20-gauge wire to the neck collar.

(b) Trim the excess wire. **Tip: Vary the placement of the coils and beads to suit your taste. This is a completely freeform design— coil and wrap as desired.**

Ride the Wave
Cuff

The extreme silhouette of this copper cuff reminds us of the natural waves of the ocean. Exaggerate the shape, as in the multicolored flower cuff, or create a gentle curve, as in the pink-and-purple bracelet. You could even try using more wires for more waves.

materials

MULTICOLORED BRACELET

3 enameled small floral components

3 enameled medium floral components

3 enameled large floral components

3 4mm flat spacer beads

21 in. 12-gauge copper wire

36 in. 20-gauge copper wire

PINK-AND-PURPLE BRACELET

3 enameled cupped floral components

3 sea glass nuggets, center-drilled

21 in. 12-gauge copper wire

36 in. 20-gauge copper wire

Note: The enameled floral components used in this project are from C-Koop Beads.

tools

Balling Wire Ends toolkit, p. 19

Brazing rod

Tape measure

Permanent marker

Heavy-duty flush cutters

Metal file

Oval bracelet mandrel

Chasing hammer

Rubber mallet

Brass brush

1.25mm metal hole punch

Finishing toolkit, p. 23 (optional)

Step 1

Cut the 12-gauge wire into three 7-in. pieces. Anneal the wire (see p. 17). Braze three ends of wire together (see p. 20). Repeat at the opposite end.

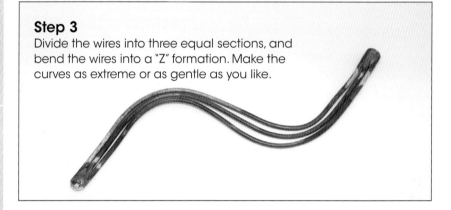

Step 2

File both ends of the brazed copper wires with a metal file until they are smooth.

Step 3

Divide the wires into three equal sections, and bend the wires into a "Z" formation. Make the curves as extreme or as gentle as you like.

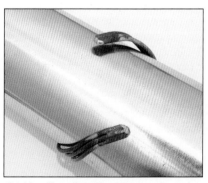

Step 4

(a) Form the wire around a bracelet mandrel at the desired size to make a cuff shape.

(b) You'll notice that the cuff ends do not meet up on the back.

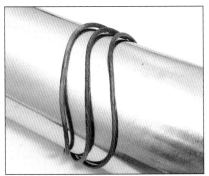

Step 5

Spread the wires apart as desired. The distance between the wires will vary, depending on the size of your curves.

Step 6

Hammer the cuff on the mandrel with the flat end of the chasing hammer to flatten the wires. Tip: The wires need to be flattened so they spread out to contain a 1.25mm hole. Hammer well.

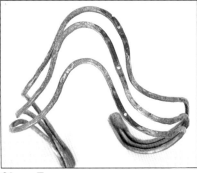

Step 7

Mark three locations on the wires for the floral components. Punch three holes in the wires at those locations. Place the cuff in a pickle solution to remove any firescale, and polish with the brass brush.

Step 8

Cut the 20-gauge wire in three 9-in. pieces. Ball one end of each wire (see p. 19). Slide beads as desired on all three wires to make components. For the Multicolored Bracelet, string a 4mm flat spacer bead followed by a small, medium, and large enameled flower on each wire. For the Pink-and-Purple Bracelet, string a sea glass nugget and a cupped enameled flower.

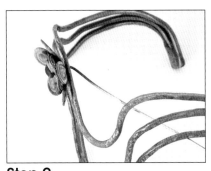

Step 9

(a) Attach the first component to the cuff by sliding the wire through the hole.

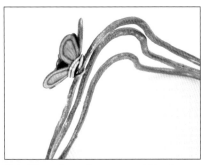

(b) Wrap the wire around the base of the component, as shown.

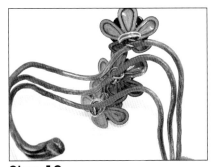

Step 10

(a) Repeat Step 9 with the two remaining components.

(b) Tumble-polish and add patina as desired (see p. 23).

The Perfect Storm
ring

Sometimes, using the same type of material can give you very different looks. In this project, which is based on the Eye of the Storm Cuff, you can choose a thin, rough disk of ancient Roman glass, or a smooth, polished sea glass nugget as your focal. Either way, you'll have a substantial ring loaded with style.

Step 1
Center the 18-gauge wire on the ring mandrel at a point that is two sizes larger than the desired finished size. Wrap two or three times around the mandrel.

Step 2
Secure the wires by crossing each end in front of the mandrel.

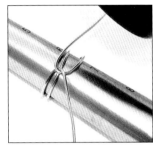

Step 3
Work-harden the wire by hammering with a rubber mallet.

materials

SEA GLASS RING
15mm center-drilled sea glass focal (see p. 12)

3½ ft. 18-gauge copper wire

12 in. 16-gauge copper wire

ROMAN GLASS RING
15mm center-drilled Roman glass focal (see p. 12)

3½ ft. 18-gauge copper wire

12 in. 16-gauge copper wire

tools
Annealing toolkit, p. 17

Measuring tape

Permanent marker

Ring mandrel

Chasing hammer

Wire cutters

Rubber mallet

Roundnose pliers

Chainnose pliers

Nylon-jaw pliers

Steel block

Awl

Finishing toolkit, p. 23 (optional)

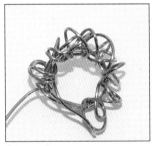

Step 4
(a) Remove the ring from the mandrel. Loosely wrap one of the wires around the ring band. Continue wrapping to the end of the wire.

(b) Place the ring on the ring mandrel, and push down to stretch the ring.

Step 5
Turn the wire end into the work with the roundnose pliers as in the Eye of the Storm Cuff, Step 5, p. 85. Trim any excess wire.

Step 6
Repeat Steps 4 and 5 with the second wire.

Step 7
Repeat Steps 4a and 4b.

Step 8
Continue hammering the ring shank and pushing it down the mandrel until it is the desired ring size.

Step 9

(a) Remove the ring from the mandrel. The width of the ring shank may be slightly uneven.

(b) To even the shank, place the ring on a steel block, and lightly hammer each side.

(c) Stop hammering when the ring shank is even on both sides.

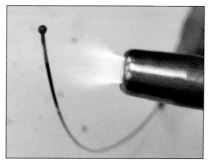

Step 10

Ball one end of the 16-gauge wire (see p. 19).

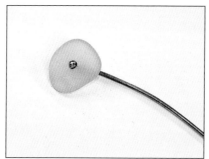

Step 11

String the focal on the wire.

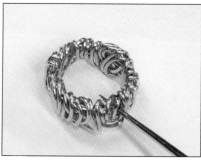

Step 12

Insert the awl into the center of the ring band to create a small gap. Insert the wire end into the gap.

Step 13

(a) Place the ring on the ring mandrel. Bring the wire end to the front.

(b) Begin wrapping the wire under the focal to create a bezel. Make as many or as few wraps as you'd like. For the Sea Glass Ring, we wrapped a full bezel around the focal. For the Roman Glass Ring, we only made a few wraps underneath the focal.

Step 14

Using the roundnose pliers, anchor the wire by wrapping around the shank. Turn the end of the wire into the work. Tumble-polish and add patina as desired (see p. 23).

Shoreline
cuff

If you like your jewelry big and bold, this is the cuff for you! Choose a weathered piece of recycled glass as your focal, or select an unusual stone or chunk of sea glass. Either way, be sure the focal element is hardy and thick, and drill two holes before beginning this project.

materials

RECYCLED GLASS CUFF

30mm (approx.) double-drilled recycled glass focal (see p. 12)

1½x6 in. 20-gauge metal blank

1½x6 in. 24-gauge metal blank

48 in. 18-gauge wire

4 ½-in. 1.3mm nailhead rivets

SEA GLASS CUFF

28x10mm (approx.) double-drilled sea glass focal

1½x6 in. 20-gauge metal blank

1x6 in. 24-gauge metal blank

48 in. 18-gauge wire

4 ½-in. 1.3mm nailhead rivets

tools

Annealing toolkit, p. 17

Texturing toolkit, p. 21

Permanent marker

Tape measure

Circle template

Metal shears

Metal file

1.5mm metal hole punch

Oval bracelet mandrel

Wire cutters

Chasing hammer

Brass brush

Finishing toolkit, p. 23 (optional)

Step 1

(a) Anneal the 24-gauge metal blank (see p. 17).

(b) Texture the metal blank (see p. 21). Re-anneal the metal blank.

Step 2

(a) With the circle template, draw a draw a half-round circle on each end of each metal blank.

(b) Trim the ends with metal shears, and file each rounded end with a metal file.

Step 3
Find the center of the 24-gauge textured metal blank, and punch two holes that line up with the drilled holes in the focal. At each end of the textured metal blank, punch two holes. These holes will be used to attach the top layer to the bottom layer. The holes should be a minimum of 1/8 in. from the edges.

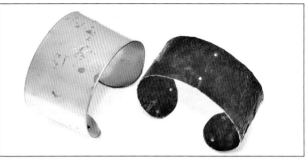

Step 4
Bend both blanks around the mandrel at the desired size. Hammer the blanks with a rubber mallet to work-harden.

Step 5
Cut two 24-in. pieces of 18-gauge wire. Ball one end of each wire (see p. 19). Slide the two wires through the holes in the focal.

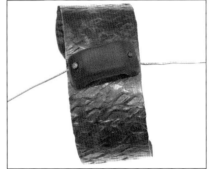

Step 6
Put the other end of the wire through the center holes on the 24-gauge textured metal blank.

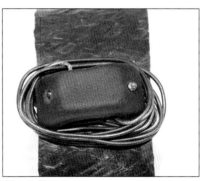

Step 7
Wrap the wire ends around the bottom of the glass in a windmill fashion. When you have the desired number of wraps, pull the wires taut, and tuck the wire ends underneath the focal.

Step 8
(a) Center the textured 24-gauge metal blank over the 20-gauge metal blank. Using the hole in the 24-gauge metal blank as a guide, punch a hole through the 20-gauge metal blank. Rivet the pieces together (see p. 22).

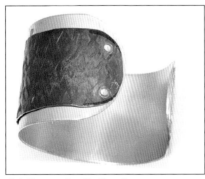

(b) Repeat with the three remaining holes. Tip: Punch holes in the 20-gauge metal one at a time to align them.

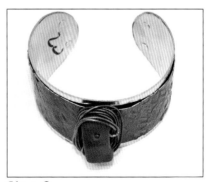

Step 9
Place the piece in the pickling solution to remove any firescale. Remove, rinse, and polish with a brass brush. Tumble-polish and add patina as desired (see p. 23).

gallery

Linda Larsen

Kim Telecky O'Neill

Melissa Cable

Steve M. Pawloski

Kim St. Jean

Linda Jereb

Acknowledgments

Thank you to our wonderful team at Kalmbach, including editor-in-chief Diane Wheeler, photographer Bill Zuback, art director Lisa Bergman, and the books marketing staff, but especially Erica Swanson, our editor, without whose support and encouragement this book would still be just a thought bubble.

Thank you to Richard LaMotte, author of *Pure Sea Glass*, for introducing the world to the beauty of sea glass.

And finally, a huge XOXO thank you to our family and friends for patiently enduring our constant state of distraction!

As a side note: After four years from conceptualization to final edit, Beth and Eva are still friends and collaborating on a second book.

About the Authors

Jewelry designer **Eva M. Sherman** began beading as a way to spend time with her daughters but soon became hopelessly addicted. In 2005, she traded in her architectural career for the opportunity to spend all her time among beads and opened Grand River Bead Studio in Cleveland, Ohio. Eva now happily spends most days in the studio creating, writing, and teaching, but has been known to take her show on the road. She has discovered an affinity for working with wire and metals, and prefers to design in an organic and unstructured style. Eva's work may be seen at *evashermandesigns.blogspot.com*.

Jewelry designer **Beth L. Martin** spends the summer months walking the beaches of Lake Erie in search of glass and other shoreline findings. In turn, these pieces become fabulous jewelry, lamps, trays, and anything else her imagination conjures up. She is well-versed in the historical lore of sea glass, as well as the mystery of its origin. Beth is continually inspired by the beautiful colors and textures of these gems. She is also an instructor, and her gift is inspiring students to incorporate sea glass in new and unique ways. Beth's work may be seen at *beachglassshop.etsy.com*.

Enhance Your Wire & Metal Skills!

Discover more projects and techniques for working with wire and metal!

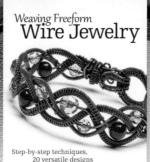

Weaving Freeform Wire Jewelry
Find 20 more compelling projects in *Weaving Freeform Wire Jewelry*. From angular, geometric forms to organic, curvy, elongated lines — and from simple flat weaves to elaborate multi-layered creations — there's no end to the potential for this technique!
#67033 • $21.99

Beautiful Wire Jewelry for Beaders 2
This all-new collection features projects that move from the basics to a comfortable challenge of increasing complexity. Discover fresh, fashionable ideas including combining copper, bronze, and silver with exciting elements like rivets and metal blanks.
#64186 • $21.95

Metal Jewelry in Bloom
Craft dogwood blossoms, orchids, daisies, and other beautiful flowers from metal, then finish them with gemstones, leather, crystals, and more. You'll learn how to cut, pierce, and texture metal, plus make cold connections including wrapping and riveting.
#64438 • $21.95

Buy now from your favorite bead or craft shop!
Or at **www.KalmbachStore.com**
or **1-800-533-6644**

Monday – Friday, 8:30 a.m. – 4:30 p.m. CST.
Outside the United States and Canada call 262-796-8776, Ext. 661.

P21823

 www.facebook.com/KalmbachJewelryBooks   www.pinterest.com/kalmbachjewelry